はじめに

グローバル社会に必要な英語プレゼンのスキル

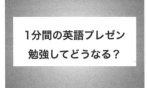

日本の社会がこの先、ますますグローバル化していくことは言うに及びません。私たちが今まで以上に異文化の人々と関わる機会が増えます。これに伴い、英語の使用頻度が高まります。本書は、こうした間近な日本の未来に備えるものです。

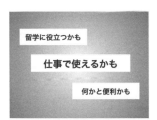

英語プレゼンテーションの技術は、「自分が意図することを異文化の相手に明確に伝える」技術です。既にグローバル化している企業や組織、その途上にあるもの、これからグローバル化していくもの、そうした所で働く皆さんに必要な技術です。

本教材はタイトルが示す通り、「1分間の英語プレゼンテーション」の技術を身につけるものです。「1分間」としているのは、短いもので気楽にたくさん経験してもらうことと、情報を短く圧縮する技術を養うことの2つの狙いがあります。

具体的には、左に示す3つの活動とプロセスで英語プレゼンテーションの技術を学んでいきます。これらは皆さんが中学・高校で学んできた英語の実践とも言えます。英語の非ネイティブ・スピーカーにも理解できる「平易な英語」の実践です。

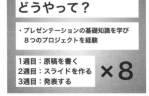

学習はプロジェクト・ベースで進められます。最初に「プレゼンテーションの基礎知識」を学び、その後、8つのプロジェクトを経験しながら段階的に仕上げていきます。皆さんの学習の成功を祈ります。

本書の出版にあたっては、松柏社の永野啓子さんに大変お世話になりました、ここに心より感謝の意を表します。

2017年 希望に満ちた春

著者 松岡 昇、傍島一夫

本書の構成と使い方

One-minute Presentation はプロジェクト・ベースの教材です。プロジェクトをひとつずつこなしながら、英語プレゼンテーションに慣れ、その技術を身につけていきます。本書の構成と使い方は以下の通りです。

1. 全体の構成：INTRODUCTIONと8つのプロジェクト

本書は以下のように、Introductionと8つのプロジェクトで構成されています。学習は **INTRODUCTION** から順に **MISSION 1**, **MISSION 2** … と進めていきます。

INTRODUCTION		英語プレゼンテーションの基礎知識と準備
MISSION 01	【個人】	INTRODUCE YOURSELF
MISSION 02	【グループ】	GIVE YOUR IDEAS: THINGS YOU ENJOY ON & OFF CAMPUS
MISSION 03	【グループ】	INTRODUCE NICE PLACES IN JAPAN
MISSION 04	【個人】	TALK ABOUT YOUR SUMMER PLANS
MISSION 05	【個人】	INTRODUCE YOUR CLASSMATES
MISSION 06	【グループ】	EXPLAIN JAPANESE CULTURE
MISSION 07	【グループ】	SOLVE PROBLEMS
MISSION 08	【個人】	TALK ABOUT YOUR FUTURE PLANS

2. INTRODUCTION：最初に学習

Introductionは「英語プレゼンテーションの基礎知識と準備」について書かれています。プロジェクトを開始する前に熟読しましょう。また、プロジェクトが開始された後も、作業を進める中で疑問等が生じた場合、適宜ページを遡り参照してください。

3. 8つのプロジェクト：個人とグループ

プロジェクトは、上の表に見る通り、個人で行うものが4つとグループで行うものが4つです。それぞれに割り当てられたテーマに従って進めてください。個人のプロジェクトの発表は1分ですが、グループでは全体で5分（各自1分、MC1分）の発表になります。

4. 各プロジェクトの構成：3週間で完結

各プロジェクトは、個人、グループに関わらず、基本的に3週間で完結します。

WEEK 1: PREPARATION 1 ▶ 準備1（主に原稿の作成）
WEEK 2: PREPARATION 2 ▶ 準備2（主にスライドの作成）
WEEK 3: PRESENTATION ▶ 発表

各週の学習内容は以下の通りです。

WEEK 1: PREPARATION 1	WEEK 2: PREPARATION 2	WEEK 3: PRESENTATION
① LEARN FROM THE SAMPLES	① PREPARE YOUR VISUAL MESSAGE	① GIVE A PRESENTATION
② LEARN WORDS, PHRASES & EXPRESSIONS	② REHEARSE	② EVALUATE YOUR OWN PRESENTATION
③ DECIDE WHAT YOU TALK ABOUT	③ HOMEWORK	③ HOMEWORK
④ PREPARE YOUR SPEECH MESSAGE		
⑤ HOMEWORK		

HOMEWORK

各Weekの最後（1回の授業の終わり）に **HOMEWORK** を指示しています。授業時間外にも時間を取って、プロジェクトの準備を進めてください。

TABLE OF CONTENTS

INTRODUCTION　　　006
英語プレゼンテーションの基礎知識と準備

MISSION 01　　　014
INTRODUCE YOURSELF
自己紹介をする

MISSION 02　　　026
GIVE YOUR IDEAS: THINGS YOU ENJOY ON & OFF CAMPUS
学生生活を有意義に過ごすアイディアを述べる

MISSION 03　　　040
INTRODUCE NICE PLACES IN JAPAN
日本の観光スポットを紹介する

MISSION 04　　　052
TALK ABOUT YOUR SUMMER PLANS
夏休みの計画について述べる

MISSION 05　　　064
INTRODUCE YOUR CLASSMATES
クラスメートを紹介する

MISSION 06　　　076
EXPLAIN JAPANESE CULTURE
日本の文化を説明する

MISSION 07　　　088
SOLVE PROBLEMS
個人や社会の問題の解決策を提案する

MISSION 08　　　100
TALK ABOUT YOUR FUTURE PLANS
将来の計画について話す

ENGLISH SKILLS	PRESENTATION SKILLS		
		INTRODUCTION	
◎平易な英語 ◎問い掛け ◎論理的な展開 ◎持ち時間と語数	◎プレゼンテーションの構造 ◎プレゼンテーションのメッセージ ◎プレゼンテーションの準備		
		MISSION 01	
◎自己紹介 ◎身分、経歴、趣味などの説明 ◎性格の描写	◎個人による初歩的な準備と発表 ◎初歩的なスライドの作成 ◎写真・イラストの活用	←	【個 人】1分
		MISSION 02	
◎楽しんでいること・取り組んでいることの説明 ◎「勧める」表現	◎グループによる初歩的な準備と発表 ◎グループでのスライド作成 ◎MCの進行 ◎グループ発表の時間管理	←	【グループ】5分
		MISSION 03	
◎観光スポットの説明 ◎文化的・歴史的背景の説明 ◎「勧める」表現	◎グループによる1つのテーマの組み立て ◎日本的なスライドの作成 ◎「手順」のスライド作成	←	【グループ】5分
		MISSION 04	
◎予定・計画の説明 ◎「予定」の表現 ◎「希望」の表現	◎個人による準備と発表 ◎時間的・物理的移動を「矢印」でスライドに表現	←	【個 人】1分
		MISSION 05	
◎人物の説明 ◎「人物紹介」の表現 ◎「印象」の描写	◎個人による準備と発表 ◎取材による内容構成 ◎スライドに強調の「図形」を利用 ◎ジョークで和みを演出	←	【個 人】1分
		MISSION 06	
◎日本の文化を説明 ◎日本独特の「もの」の説明 ◎抽象概念の説明	◎グループによる準備と発表 ◎写真、イラストの活用 ◎チャートをスライドに利用 ◎スライド上の写真に文字を書き込む技術	←	【グループ】5分
		MISSION 07	
◎個人・社会問題を「議論」 ◎論理的な展開の表現 ◎解決策「提案」の表現	◎グループでの論理的な展開 ◎説明的なスライドの作成 ◎スライドに「描画」の利用	←	【グループ】5分
		MISSION 08	
◎計画や夢を説明 ◎「職業」の語彙、表現 ◎「願望・夢」の表現	◎個人による準備と発表 ◎時系列で説明的なスライドの作成 ◎スライドにアニメーションの活用	←	【個 人】1分

― INTRODUCTION ―
英語プレゼンテーションの基礎知識と準備

プロジェクトを始める前に、まずはプレゼンテーションの基礎知識と準備について学びましょう。以下のような項目について確認していきます。

プレゼンテーションの基礎知識

① プレゼンテーションの構造　　② プレゼンテーションのメッセージ

プレゼンテーションの準備

① 内容を考える　　② 骨組みを作る　　③ 原稿を書く
④ スライドを作る　⑤ リハーサルを行う　⑥ 配布資料を準備する

1　プレゼンテーションの基礎知識

「プレゼンテーション」とは、自分の考えや情報を複数の人たちに発表する行為で、英語では次のように定義できます。

> **A presentation is a way of giving information <u>to a group of people</u>, usually <u>in a formal way</u>.**

プレゼンテーションが一般の「話」と異なるところは **to a group of people**、つまり「何人もの聞き手」が話の対象であり、さらに **in a formal way**、つまり、その話を「正式な方法で」行うという2点です。このため、プレゼンテーションを成功させるためには、しかるべき技術や方法が求められます。

1 プレゼンテーションの構造

聴衆に伝わりやすいプレゼンテーションにするためには、自分の考えや情報を整理して、聴衆が理解しやすい構成で話すことが重要です。一般に、プレゼンテーションは大きく序論、本論、結論という3つのパートから構成されます。

---

1. 序論　INTRODUCTION
挨拶、興味を引きつける、話題と目的、概観（overview）

2. 本論　BODY
論点1：主要文＋説明（例、経験、事実、理由、引用など）
　＋つなぎ
論点2：主要文＋説明（例、経験、事実、理由、引用など）
　＋つなぎ
論点3：主要文＋説明（例、経験、事実、理由、引用など）
　＋つなぎ

3. 結論　CONCLUSION
まとめ（wrap-up）、終わりの挨拶

---

1. 序論 … INTRODUCTION

序論では挨拶や自己紹介を行い、続いてプレゼンテーションの主題やその目的を伝えます。最後に、プレゼンテーションの概観（overview）を示します。概観は本に例えるなら「目次」で、聴衆に前もって話の道筋を示します。

2. 本論 … BODY

本論では自分の考えや情報を具体的かつ詳細に伝えます。本論はいくつかの論点で構成され、それぞれの論点は主要文（topic sentence）に始まり、詳細を説明する文（supporting sentences）がそれに続きます。論点と論点の間は適切なつなぎ（transition）の言葉を使って橋渡しをします。

3. 結論 … CONCLUSION

結論では、今までの話の要点をまとめたり（wrap-up）、特に重要な事柄を繰り返し強調したりすることで聴衆の理解を確認します。最後に挨拶をしてプレゼンテーション全体を締めくくります。

② プレゼンテーションのメッセージ

プレゼンテーションには3種類のメッセージがあります。言葉によるメッセージ、つまり、スピーチ・メッセージと視覚的メッセージ、そして身体的メッセージです。これら3種類のメッセージを効果的に使うことが、プレゼンテーションの成功につながります。

スピーチメッセージ【SPEECH】	視覚的メッセージ【VISUAL】	身体的メッセージ【PHYSICAL】
① 平易な英語	① スライド（PowerPoint）	① 声の抑揚
② 問い掛け	② 書画カメラ	（強弱、高低、長短）
③ 論理的な展開	③ ホワイトボード	② アイ・コンタクト：5秒
④ おもしろい	④ フリップカード	③ 手、ポインター
	⑤ 現物	④ 姿勢

1. スピーチ【SPEECH】メッセージ

スピーチ・メッセージは私たちの話す言葉（英語）そのものです。ポイントは以下の4つです。

1 平易な英語
聴衆にとっていかにわかり易い言葉（平易な英語）で話すかが何より重要です。平易な語彙と構文、短めの文（15語前後）で原稿を書きましょう。

2 問い掛け
聴衆の注意を引きつけるためには、時折、聴衆に問い掛けて、対話をしているかのような雰囲気を作ることが大切です。原稿に「問い掛け」を入れましょう。

3 論理的な展開
聴衆の理解を得るためには論理的である必要があります。聴衆の抱く"Why"や"How"に答えるような話の展開になるよう、十分に原稿を練りましょう。

4 面白い内容(Interesting/Funny)
話の内容が面白くなければ聴衆は耳を傾けてくれません。興味を抱かせる原稿を書きましょう。また、ときにはジョークで笑わせることも必要です。

2. 視覚的【VISUAL】メッセージ

視覚的メッセージは視覚的補助（visual aids）と呼ばれ、スピーチ・メッセージを補助するものです。コンピュータのソフト（例：PowerPoint）によるスライドの他に、書画カメラ、ホワイトボード、フリップカード、現物などがあります。最も使用頻度の高いスライドについてポイントを挙げましょう。

1 キーワードと数字（Key Words/Numbers）

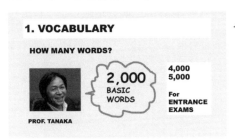
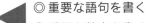

◎ 重要な語句を書く
◎ 重要な数字を書く
◎ 文は書かない

2 画像（Photos, Illustrations）

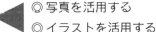

◎ 写真を活用する
◎ イラストを活用する

3 図表・グラフ（Charts/Graphs）

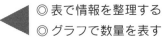

◎ 表で情報を整理する
◎ グラフで数量を表す

3. 身体的【PHYSICAL】メッセージ

身体的メッセージも視覚的メッセージと同じくらいスピーチ・メッセージの助けになります。身体的メッセージには以下の4つがあります。

1 声の抑揚（Voice Inflection）
声の抑揚とは声の強弱、高低、長短のことです。私たち日本人は英語を平坦に発音しがちです。ややオーバーに感情を注ぎ込んで抑揚を大きくしましょう。

2 アイ・コンタクト（Eye Contact）
聴衆に話しかけるときには目を合わせること（アイ・コンタクト）が欠かせません。一人ひとりに5秒程度のアイ・コンタクトをとって話しましょう。

3 手、ポインター (Hands, Pointer)

手やポインターでスライドの一部を指して注意を喚起したり、言葉の意味を増幅したり補足したりすることができます。積極的に使いましょう。

4 姿勢 (Posture)

体は堂々とした姿勢で、正面を常に聴衆に向けることが大事です。体の向きと口と目を一緒にして、メッセージを聴衆に届けましょう。

2 プレゼンテーションの準備

プレゼンテーションの準備は以下の順序と要領で行います。

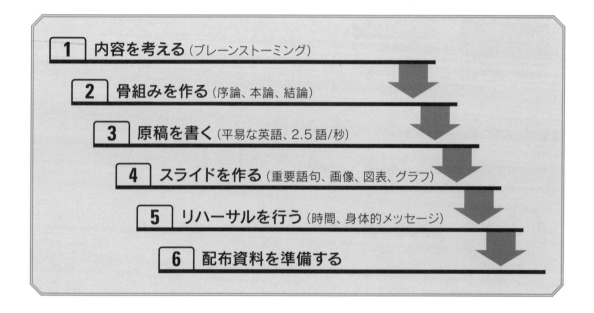

❶ 内容を考える

プレゼンテーションの内容（論点）を決めるためにブレーンストーミングを行います。ブレーンストーミングとは、脳 (brain) に嵐 (storm) を起こして、既成概念にとらわれないアイディアを創出する思考方法です。

1 白紙を準備し (Wordで作成しても可)、プレゼンテーションのテーマに対し思いつくことを書き出します。
2 出尽くした頃を見て、内容の関連からグループを作ります。このグループが論点になります。
3 それぞれのグループに見出しをつけ、話す順番を決めます。

❷ 骨組みを作る

プレゼンテーションの持ち時間と、❶のブレーンストーミングの結果得られた論点の数から、時間の配分、原稿の語数（2.5語/秒）、センテンス数（1文＝15語）を概算し、下のような表（Wordで作成しても可）で骨組みを作ります。

【個人の例】MISSION 04: Sample 1 ＝ 持ち時間1分（60秒）、論点2つ

		内　容	時間配分	語数	センテンス数
序　論			0'10"	25語	2文
本論	POINT 1	アルバイト	0'20"	50語	3～4文
	POINT 2	北海道旅行	0'20"	50語	3～4文
結　論			0'10"	25語	2文

【グループの例】MISSION 07 ＝ 持ち時間5分、論点4つ

		内　容	担当	時間配分	語数	センテンス数
序　論		現　状	MC	0'15"	25語	2文
本論	POINT 1	語　彙	和也	1'00"	150語	10文
		transition	MC	0'10"	25語	2文
	POINT 2	文　法	茜	1'00"	150語	10文
		transition	MC	0'10"	25語	2文
	POINT 3	Speaking練習	美優	1'00"	150語	10文
		transition	MC	0'10"	25語	2文
	POINT 4	Listening練習	琢磨	1'00"	150語	10文
結　論			MC	0'15"	25語	2文

❸ 原稿を書く

「骨組み」を元に、スピーチ原稿を作成します。書くに当たっては、以下の5つの点に注意しましょう。

1 平易な英語で：平易な語彙と構文で書く。
2 短い文で：1文が15語前後の文で書く。
3 小さい段落で：1段落を5文前後で構成する。
4 話の展開：内容に応じて、時系列（過去 ➡ 現在 ➡ 未来）、重要度順（重要度が低い ➡ 重要度が高い、または、高い ➡ 低い）、論理的配列のいずれかに従って進める。
5 面白い内容：深刻な話でなければジョークの1つや2つを入れてみる。

❹ スライドを作る

コンピュータのソフト（例：PowerPoint）を使って、プレゼンテーションを効果的かつ印象的にするスライドを作成しましょう。

🔳 スライドの構成と枚数：

個人の場合：1分間なのでOVERVIEWやWRAP-UPはなくても可。

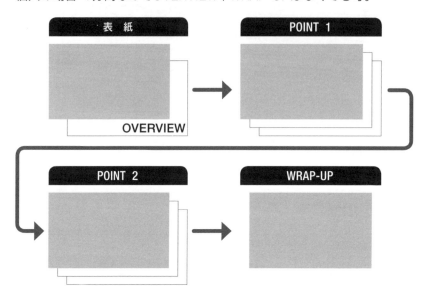

グループの場合：全体で5分間なのでOVERVIEWとWRAP-UPは必要

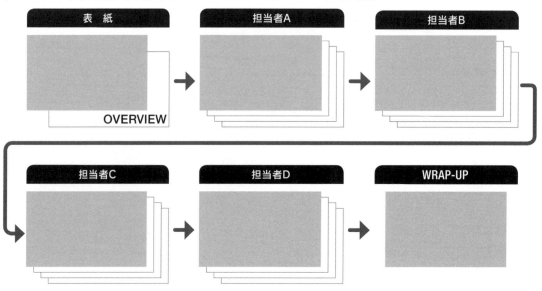

🔳 スライドの内容： ➡ P.8の「視覚的メッセージ【VISUAL】」を参照

❺ リハーサルを行う

リハーサルは準備の最終確認であり、同時に本番のための練習です。
以下の要領でリハーサルを行いましょう。

1 時計を使ってタイミングを計る
持ち時間を守るのはプレゼンテーションで最も大事なマナーです。
リハーサルには必ず時計を使い、秒単位でタイミングを計りましょう。

2 聞き手の前で
クラスメートや友人の協力を得て、聞き手の前でリハーサルを行いましょう。
新鮮な耳と目で感じたコメントがもらえます。

3 修正する
リハーサルの結果、修正すべき文言やスライド、あるいは時間配分があれば修正しましょう。

4 自分の言葉になるまで
原稿を手に持ってプレゼンテーションすることは厳禁です。
Wordで作成した原稿は、PowerPointの「ノート」に貼りつけ、それを「ノート」モードでプリント・アウトします。このプリントを発表までの数日間持ち歩き、スライドの部分をチラッと見るだけでセリフが出てくるまで練習しましょう。

❻ 配布資料を準備する

PowerPoint のスライドなどを利用して配布資料を作成し、発表の際、聴衆に配布できるように準備しましょう。

HOMEWORK
① MISSION 1のサンプル・プレゼンテーションを読む。
② LEARN WORDS, PHRASES & EXPRESSIONS（P.19）に目を通す。
③ 自己紹介の内容を考えてくる。

MISSION 01 では…

自己紹介を通じてプレゼンテーションの練習をします。
自分自身のことをよく知ってもらえるように、
自分に関する情報をうまくまとめ、印象的に伝わるように工夫しましょう。

CAN-DO LIST

ENGLISH SKILLS

- 自己紹介について英語で原稿を準備し、口頭で発表することができる。
- 自分の身分、経歴、趣味、性格について英語で描写ができる。
- 自己紹介に必要な英語の表現（I'm a first-year student, majoring in...）などが使える。

PRESENTATION SKILLS

- 初歩的なプレゼンテーションが個人でできる。
- 内容と時間からプレゼンテーションを適切に構成できる。
- スライド作成の基礎を学習し、写真やイラストを効果的に使える。

WEEK 1 PREPARATION 1

プロジェクトの内容と準備の要領を確認し、**WEEK1** の準備を行います。

" MISSION 01 "
INTRODUCE YOURSELF

設定 ▶ 留学生が在籍するクラスでの初日
目的 ▶ 自分に関する情報(名前、出身地、趣味、性格など)を伝え、自分について知ってもらう。
形態 ▶ 個人
時間 ▶ 1分
準備 ▶ **WEEK 1** … サンプルを読む、語彙・表現を学ぶ、原稿を書く。
　　　WEEK 2 … スライドを作成し、リハーサルを行う。
　　　WEEK 3 … 発表する。

LEARN FROM THE SAMPLES

SAMPLE 1   Audio 02

▶ Hello. My name is Kenta Shimada but my friends call me Ken. I'm a first-year student, majoring in Japanese literature.

▶ Now, I'm going to talk about (1) where I'm from, (2) my hobbies, and (3) my personality.

▶ I was born and raised in Fukuoka. This is my house in Fukuoka, where my parents and a younger sister live now. I moved to Nagoya this spring. I live in this apartment alone. It's smaller than my house in Fukuoka, but very comfortable.

▶ I like watching movies and reading books, but my No.1 hobby is soccer. I like watching professional soccer games. Does anyone here support any particular team? I'm a big fan of Nagoya Grampus.

▶ I'm a very sociable person. I never find it difficult to make friends.

▶ Well, nice meeting you all. I hope to make many friends here in this class.

SAMPLE 2 🔊 Audio 03

▶ Hello everyone. My name is Misaki Okada. I'd like to introduce myself.

▶ I'm from Yamanashi prefecture, which is famous for Mt. Fuji. It was registered as a World Heritage Site in 2013, but I've never climbed it.

▶ There're four people in my family: my parents, a younger brother and myself. Oh, one more member — our dog, Tamano-fuji. I love them all.

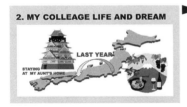

▶ I moved to Osaka last year to enter the university and I'm staying at my aunt's home.

▶ I'm a member of the *kyudo* club. We meet and practice twice a week. I'm dreaming of becoming a champion at the National Athletic Meet.

▶ Once a week, I take a cooking class. I want to learn how to make delicious meals for myself and my future family. It was hard at first, but I'm getting better little by little.

▶ In the future, I'd like to work for an airline company as a ground staff member. Thank you.

LEARN WORDS, PHRASES & EXPRESSIONS

プロジェクトに使えそうな語句や表現を学び、原稿作成に活用しましょう。

WORDS & PHRASES

1 出身地・居住地
I was born and grew up in … / My hometown is … / I'm from … /
I come from … / move to … / I live in an apartment / condominium /
school dormitory

2 大学・科目
be in the first year / be in the second year / a first-year student /
a second-year student / Law Department / The Department of Economics /
major / major in … / a business major / Japanese literature / education /
phycology / politics / biology / science & technology / chemistry

3 趣味
hobby / favorite pastime / play computer games / watch movies /
go shopping / practice karate / play the piano / make sweets /
listen to music / read comics

4 性格
sociable / friendly / outgoing / kind / honest / reliable / patient / active / quiet /
cheerful / shy / polite / serious / funny / entertaining / talkative / lazy / responsible

EXPRESSIONS

1「名前」
My name is … / I am … / My friends call me … / Please call me …

2「学年・専攻科目」
I'm a first-year student / I'm in the first year / I'm a freshman / My major is … /
I major in … / I study … / required subject / elective course

3「趣味」
My hobbies are … / I like to … / I like ~ing / I love ~ing /
My favorite pastime is … / I usually spend my free time reading books /
I'm into … / I enjoy ~ing

PRESENTATION TECHNIQUES
" 番号をつける "

SAMPLE 1 の第2ブロック Now, I'm going to talk about (1) where I'm from, (2) my hobbies and (3) my personality.	複数の事項を列挙する際に I'm going to talk about (1) … (2) … and (3) … のように番号をつけて話すと、聴衆の聞くべきポイントがより明確になります。(1)、(2)、(3)はそれぞれ one, two, three と読み上げます。

DECIDE WHAT YOU TALK ABOUT

サンプル・プレゼンテーションを参考にブレーンストーミングを行い、あなた自身のプレゼンテーションの内容を決めましょう（下の【あなたのプレゼンテーション】にメモ）。

【SAMPLE1のプレゼンテーション】		【あなたのプレゼンテーション】	
タイトル	自己紹介		
背 景	名前 ニックネーム 学年・専攻		
Point 1 住 居	出身地と自宅 名古屋に引っ越した 今のアパート：狭いが快適		
Point 2 趣 味	映画鑑賞と読書が好き 一番の趣味はサッカー サッカーは見る方が好き グランパスの大ファン		
Point 3 性 格	社交的な性格 友達はすぐできる		
CONCLUSION	挨拶		

PREPARE YOUR SPEECH MESSAGE

【あなたのプレゼンテーション】を元に、原稿を作成しましょう（パソコンのWordに直接書き込んでも可）。

1 主要な英文を作成しましょう。

▼「出身地・居住地」について
  I was born and grew up in … / I live in … などを使って

▼「趣味」について
　My hobbies are ... / I like doing 〜 などを使って

▼「性格」について
　I'm very ... and ... などを使って

2 作成した主要な英文を中心に枝葉をつけて、INTRODUCTION, BODY, CONCLUSIONの構成を整えて、原稿全体(150語前後)を完成させましょう。

3 原稿の点検
　作成した原稿(Speech Message)を「点検リスト」でチェックしましょう。

SPEECH MESSAGEの点検	点検のポイント	チェック
① Number of Words	時間に対して語数は適量か	☐
② Plain English	平易な英語で書かれているか	☐
③ Rhetorical Questions	聴衆への問い掛けはあるか	☐
④ Logical	論理的に書かれているか	☐
⑤ Interesting (Funny)	興味深い内容になっているか	☐

HOMEWORK

① 原稿が未完成の場合は完成させ、点検する。
② 次回のスライド作成のための材料(写真、イラストなど)を準備する。

WEEK 2　PREPARATION 2

WEEK2の準備をします。スライドを作成し、リハーサルを行います。
また、発表の際の配布資料を準備します。

PREPARE YOUR VISUAL MESSAGE

1 スライドの作成

サンプル・プレゼンテーションのスライドを参考に、あなた自身のスライドを原稿と照らし合わせながら作成しましょう。

【SAMPLE1のスライドの構成と内容】

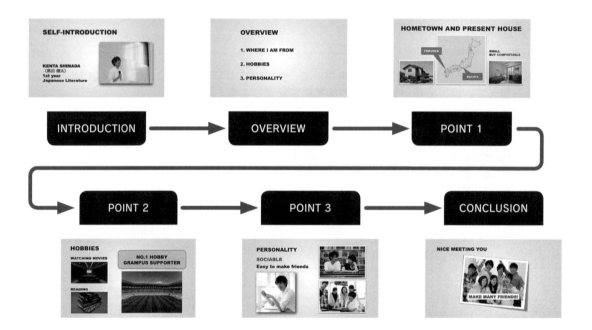

2 今回のプロジェクトでの工夫：文字と写真で基本的なスライドを作る。

スライド上にキーワード（数字）と写真（イラスト）を載せて、プレゼンターの話を効果的に補助するスライドを作りましょう。写真はツールバーから［挿入］→［画像］→［保存先］から取り込みます。

Now, I'm going to talk about (1) where I'm from, (2) my hobbies, and (3) my personality.

キーとなるワードや数字

I like **watching movies** and **reading** books, but my **No.1 hobby** is soccer. (中略) I'm a big fan of **Nagoya Grampus**.

理解を助ける写真やイラスト

3 スライドの点検

作成したスライド（Visual Message）を「点検リスト」でチェックしましょう。

VISUAL MESSAGE の点検	点検のポイント	チェック
① Number of Slides	スライドの枚数は適当か	☐
② Key Words/Numbers	重要な語句や数字は書かれているか	☐
③ Images (Photos, Illustrations)	写真やイラストは効果的に使えているか	☐
④ Charts/Graphs	図表やグラフは効果的に使えているか	☐

REHEARSE

以下の要領でリハーサルをしましょう。

1 原稿を覚える

自分のPCでスライドを見ながら（ツールバーで［スライドショー］）原稿を覚える。1回目、2回目と回数を重ねるごとに原稿から目を離し、スライドだけをヒントに英語が口をついて出てくるまで練習を繰り返す。

2 ペア練習 （A：プレゼンター、B：聞き手）

ペアを組んで各自3回リハーサルを行う。プレゼンターは自分のPCでスライドを見せながら発表し、聞き手は「点検リスト」でプレゼンターのパフォーマンスをチェックする（スマホなどでビデオ撮影をしてもよい）。

	A	B
1回目	発 表	Aが話す英語（Speech Message）に焦点をあてコメントする
2回目	発 表	スライド（Visual Message）に焦点をあてコメントする
3回目	発 表	声、目、手、姿勢（Physical Message）に焦点をあてコメントする

引き続きAとBは役割を換え、同様の練習を行う。

MISSION 01

点検項目	評 価					コメント
❶ SPEECH MESSAGE	1	2	3	4	5	
Plain English	1	2	3	4	5	
Rhetorical Questions	1	2	3	4	5	
Logical	1	2	3	4	5	
Interesting (Funny)	1	2	3	4	5	
❷ VISUAL MESSAGE (Slides)	1	2	3	4	5	
Key Words/Numbers	1	2	3	4	5	
Images (Photos, Illustrations)	1	2	3	4	5	
Charts/Graphs	1	2	3	4	5	
❸ PHYSICAL MESSAGE	1	2	3	4	5	
Voice Inflection	1	2	3	4	5	
Eye Contact	1	2	3	4	5	
Hands (Pointer)	1	2	3	4	5	
Posture	1	2	3	4	5	

MAKE HANDOUTS

発表の際、聴衆に配布する資料(PowerPointのスライドを使った配布資料)を以下の要領で準備しましょう。

❶ PowerPointのツールバーから[ファイル] ➡ [印刷]をクリック
❷ [設定:フルページサイズのスライド]脇の▼をクリック
❸ [9スライド(横)]を選択 ➡ [印刷]

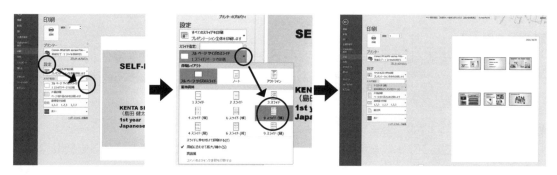

HOMEWORK

① リハーサルの結果、修正の必要があれば修正する。
② 原稿を見ずにスラスラ言えるようになるまで練習する。
③ 発表用の配布資料を準備する。

WEEK 3 PRESENTATION

プロジェクトの発表を行います。発表の後に自己評価をしましょう。

GIVE A PRESENTATION

☐ 配付資料を配る。
☐ 原稿を見ずに発表を行う。
☐ 制限時間(1分)内に全体を収める。
☐ 発表前にスマホ等によるビデオ撮影をクラスメートに依頼する。

EVALUATE YOUR OWN PRESENTATION

撮った映像を見て自己評価をし、次のステップアップにつなげましょう。

評価項目	評価					コメント
❶ SPEECH MESSAGE	1	2	3	4	5	
Plain English	1	2	3	4	5	
Rhetorical Questions	1	2	3	4	5	
Logical	1	2	3	4	5	
Interesting (Funny)	1	2	3	4	5	
❷ VISUAL MESSAGE (Slides)	1	2	3	4	5	
Key Words/Numbers	1	2	3	4	5	
Images (Photos, Illustrations)	1	2	3	4	5	
Charts/Graphs	1	2	3	4	5	
❸ PHYSICAL MESSAGE	1	2	3	4	5	
Voice Inflection	1	2	3	4	5	
Eye Contact	1	2	3	4	5	
Hands (Pointer)	1	2	3	4	5	
Posture	1	2	3	4	5	

特記事項

HOMEWORK

① MISSION 2のサンプル・プレゼンテーションを読む。
② LEARN WORDS, PHRASES & EXPRESSIONS (P.32)に目を通す。
③ 学生生活で楽しんでいることや取り組んでいることについてまとめておく。

MISSION 02
GIVE YOUR IDEAS: THINGS YOU ENJOY ON & OFF CAMPUS

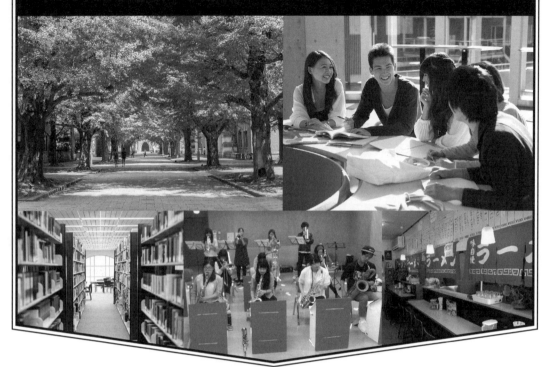

MISSION 02 では…

学生生活を有意義に過ごすためのアイディアを各自の経験から述べ、
クラスメートに勧めるプロジェクトです。
あなたの楽しんでいること、熱心に取り組んでいることなどを
グループで発表しましょう。

CAN-DO LIST

ENGLISH SKILLS

- 自分の楽しんでいることや取り組んでいることを英語で説明できる。
- 「勧める」表現(I'd recommend ... など)ができる。
- グループとしてまとまりのある内容を英語で表現できる。

PRESENTATION SKILLS

- グループ・プレゼンテーションの準備と発表ができる。
- 各自の作成したスライドをグループとしてひとつにまとめることができる。
- グループ発表の時間管理ができる。

WEEK 1　PREPARATION 1

プロジェクトの内容と準備の要領を確認し、**WEEK1** の準備を行います。

" MISSION 02 "
GIVE YOUR IDEAS: THINGS YOU ENJOY ON & OFF CAMPUS

設定 ▶ 留学生が在籍するクラス
目的 ▶ 学生生活を有意義に過ごすアイディアを各自の経験から述べ、クラスメートに勧める。
形態 ▶ グループ（4人）
時間 ▶ 5分（グループで）
準備 ▶ **WEEK 1** … サンプルを読む、語彙・表現を学ぶ、グループで打ち合わせる、原稿を書く。
　　　　WEEK 2 … スライドを作成し、グループで1つにまとめる、リハーサルを行う。
　　　　WEEK 3 … グループで発表する。

LEARN FROM THE SAMPLE Audio 04

SAMPLE

▶ **MC(Keisuke):** Hello, everybody. We are Group 4, and I'm Keisuke Yamada, leader of the group.

▶ **MC(Keisuke):** I know you're all busy with classes and homework every day. Still you have something that you particularly enjoy on and off campus. Now, we, Group 4 people, will tell you what each of us enjoys. First, Rie will talk about her club. Second, Tsuyoshi will tell you about his language study. After that, I'll talk about my part-time job. And finally, Yuko will tell you how she enjoys her time in the school library. Rie, will you begin?

MISSION 02

▶ **Rie:** Sure. Does anyone here belong to a club or a circle? I'm a member of a jazz orchestra called Cool Birds. It's a really cool band. I heard them play at the new student welcoming event in spring, and I immediately decided to join them. In fact, I played the trombone in a brass band when I was in high school.

▶ I'm not a regular member yet. You have to be really good to get a regular position. Therefore, most of the regular players are 2nd– and 3rd–year students. First-year students like me have to spend a year practicing on their own.

▶ We take part in the All Japan Collegiate Jazz Contest in summer, perform at the school festival in fall, and have an annual concert in December.

▶ I really look forward to playing in front of you some day.

MC(Keisuke): Thank you, Rie. We hope she gets a regular position and plays for us in the near future.

▶ Now, Tsuyoshi. He enjoys language study.

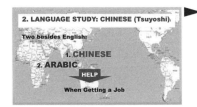

Tsuyoshi: As Keisuke said, I'm interested in foreign languages. I'm thinking of learning two languages besides English: Chinese and Arabic. I believe these will surely help me when I get a job.

Now I'm taking a basic Chinese course. It's easier than I thought. Look at this. You can guess the meaning, right?

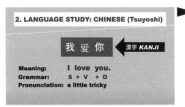

Yes, it means "I love you." It's easy because we can understand kanji characters. How about the grammar? S + V + O – the same as English. So, for us, Chinese is an easy language to learn. The pronunciation is a little tricky, though.

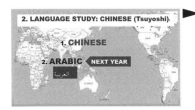

Why don't you take a Chinese class, too? I think I'll take Arabic next year.

MC(Keisuke): Wow, he is such a serious student! 谢谢, Tsuyoshi.
By the way, how many of you have a part-time job? Working part-time is another important thing we university students do, right?

Keisuke: Look! This is where I work. It's a ramen shop and I work here three days a week from 5:30 to 9:30.

► My job is mainly to help the chef in the kitchen, but I often go out of the kitchen and take orders from customers and serve them when we're busy.

► A good thing about this job is that I can get a *makanai*, or a free meal, after work. This really helps me save money. I also can learn how to cook.

► Sometimes, we have foreign customers. I'm not very good at English, but I always have to take care of them because no one else can speak English. I explain the menu and take orders. It's not easy, but I'm getting better.

► **MC (Keisuke):** Working part-time is not just for money, but we learn a lot of things that we can't at school, right?
Now, our last speaker, Yuko. Her favorite place on campus is the library.

► **Yuko:** Hi, friends. Do you ever go to the school library? Do you go there to study or to read books? Of course, a library is a place where you study and read books, but here's the way I like to spend my time there.

▶ As you know, our school library has an audio-visual section on the 3rd floor. You'll find hundreds of CDs, DVDs, and VHS videos.

▶ And you can enjoy music, movies, *rakugo* and stuff like that in a quiet booth.

▶ I like classical music, so I often go there and watch concerts and operas on DVDs. The sound and pictures are so beautiful that I always have a wonderful experience. If you've never been there, why don't you take some time and have a look around? I'm sure you'll find something you like.

▶ **MC(Keisuke):** Sounds great! Thank you, Yuko.

Now, let's wrap up. We, Group 4 people, enjoy different things …

Rie: I'm in a big band and enjoy jazz …
Tsuyoshi: I like languages and enjoy studying Chinese now …
Keisuke: I work part-time at a ramen shop, where I learn lots of things …
Yuko: and I enjoy my time in the school library.
MC(Keisuke): We hope our presentation will help you enjoy your university lives. Thank you.

LEARN WORDS, PHRASES & EXPRESSIONS

プロジェクトに使えそうな語句や表現を学び、原稿作成に活用しましょう。

WORDS & PHRASES

1 クラブ・サークル
I'm a member of ... / I'm in a rock band. / tennis circle / baseball team / volunteer group / *rakugo* study group / play soccer / practice *karate*

2 アルバイト
work part-time at ... / have a part-time job / work at a convenience store / three days a week / work from 6:00 to 9:00 p.m. / teach children at a *juku* school

3 勉強
be interested in foreign languages / go to bookkeeping school / get a qualification / study for the TOEIC® test / take part in an internship program at ...

4 その他
hang out with friends / make friends / read books / enjoy talking in the cafeteria / have a *go-kon*, or a group blind date / My favorite place on campus is ...

EXPRESSIONS

1 「楽しんでいる・取り組んでいる」
I enjoy ~ ing ... / I'm studying ... / I work part-time at ... two days a week. / We are working hard in a volunteer group to help ...

2 「勧める・勧める理由」
I'd recommend ... / Why don't you ...? / You should ... / How about ...? / You can enjoy ... / You can learn ... / It's a lot of fun. / A good thing about ... is that ....

PRESENTATION TECHNIQUES
" MC（司会進行役）の英語 "

1 First, Rie will talk about .... **Second**, Tsuyoshi will tell you about .... **After that**, I'll talk about .... **And finally**, Yuko will tell you	▶ グループ・プレゼンテーションでは、メンバーの1人がMC役を務めます。MCは発表の冒頭で左のようにプレゼンターと話題を紹介します。
2 Rie, will you begin? / Thank you, Rie. / Now, Tsuyoshi. He'll talk about ... / Thanks. / Now, our last speaker, Yuko. Her favorite place is ...	▶ また、MCは、左のようにプレゼンターとプレゼンターの橋渡し (transition) をし、進行をスムーズに進めると同時に、聴衆に話の「道案内」をします。

DECIDE WHAT YOU TALK ABOUT

サンプル・プレゼンテーションを参考に、以下の要領で内容を決めましょう。

1 リーダー（グループのまとめ役）とMC（master of ceremony: 司会進行役）を決める。
2 MCは進行役に加え、自分のTOPICも担当する。
3 グループ内でTOPICが偏らないように協議し、各自が話す内容をきめる。
4 決まった内容を下の表に記入し、グループで共有する。

【サンプル・プレゼンテーション】

	内　容	担　当	時　間
INTRODUCTION	Greeting / Overview	MC	0'15"
TOPIC 1	Club: Jazz Orchestra	理　恵	1'00"
	transition	MC	0'10"
TOPIC 2	Language Study: Chinese	剛	1'00"
	transition	MC	0'10"
TOPIC 3	Part-Time Job: Ramen Shop	啓　介	1'00"
	transition	MC	0'10"
TOPIC 4	School Library: Concerts & Operas	優　子	1'00"
CONCLUSION	Wrap-Up / Greeting	MC 全員	0'15"

【あなたのグループのプレゼンテーション】

	内　容	担　当	時　間
INTRODUCTION	Greeting / Overview	MC	0'15"
TOPIC 1			1'00"
	transition	MC	0'10"
TOPIC 2			1'00"
	transition	MC	0'10"
TOPIC 3			1'00"
	transition	MC	0'10"
TOPIC 4			1'00"
CONCLUSION	Wrap-Up / Greeting	MC 全員	0'15"

PREPARE YOUR SPEECH MESSAGE

【あなたのグループのプレゼンテーション】を元に、原稿を作成しましょう（パソコンのWordに直接書き込んでも可）。

1 主要な英文を作成しましょう。

▼「楽しんでいる・取り組んでいること」について：
  I enjoy ... / I'm a member of ... などを使って

```
[                                                              ]
```

▼「勧める」について：
  I'd recommend ... / Why don't you ...? などを使って

```
[                                                              ]
```

▼「勧める理由」について：
  You can enjoy ... / It's a lot of fun. などを使って

```
[                                                              ]
```

2 作成した主要な英文を中心に枝葉をつけて、自分の担当箇所の原稿（150語前後）を完成させましょう。

3 原稿の点検

作成した原稿（Speech Message）を下のリストで点検しましょう。

SPEECH MESSAGE の点検	点検のポイント	チェック
① Number of Words	時間に対して語数は適量か	☐
② Plain English	平易な英語で書かれているか	☐
③ Rhetorical Questions	聴衆への問い掛けはあるか	☐
④ Logical	論理的に書かれているか	☐
⑤ Interesting (Funny)	興味深い内容になっているか	☐

4 MC担当者は進行のための原稿も準備しましょう。

◎【あなたのグループのプレゼンテーション】を元に、
　グループ全体のINTRODUCTIONとCONCLUSIONの原稿を準備する。
◎【あなたのグループのプレゼンテーション】を元に、プレゼンターとプレゼンターの橋渡し
　(transition)の原稿も準備する（P.32のPRESENTATION TECHNIQUESを参照）。

HOMEWORK

① 原稿が未完成の場合は完成させ、点検する。
② 次回のスライド作成のための材料（写真、イラストなど）を準備する。

WEEK 2　PREPARATION 2

WEEK2 の準備をします。スライドを作成し、リハーサルを行います。

PREPARE YOUR VISUAL MESSAGE

1 スライドの構成と内容
グループ全体と各自のパートの両方を考えながらスライドを作成しましょう。

【サンプル・プレゼンテーションの例】

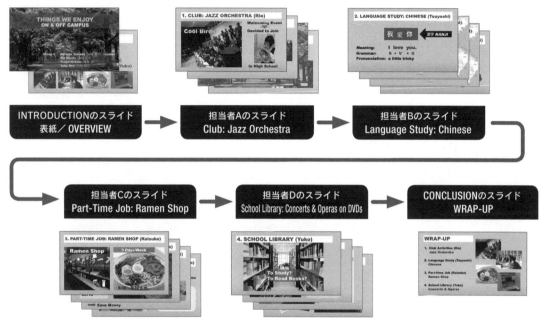

2 スライドの作成
◎作業を始める前にグループ内でスライドのデザインを統一する。
◎各自が別々に自分の担当するパートのスライドを作成する。
◎INTRODUCTIONとCONCLUSIONのスライドは手分けして作成する。

3 今回のプロジェクトでの工夫：「つなぎのスライド」を作る
MCが次のプレゼンターを紹介するときの「つなぎのスライド」を準備しましょう。OVERVIEWのスライドをコピーし、次のプレゼンターの部分だけ目立つようにします。

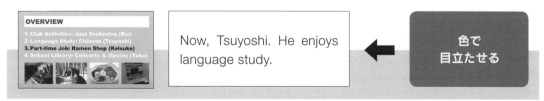

4 スライドの点検

作成したスライド（Visual Message）を「点検リスト」で点検しましょう。

VISUAL MESSAGE の点検	点検のポイント	チェック
① Number of Slides	スライドの枚数は適当か	☐
② Key Words/Numbers	重要な語句や数字は書かれているか	☐
③ Images (Photos, Illustrations)	写真やイラストは効果的に使えているか	☐
④ Charts / Graphs	図表やグラフは効果的に使えているか	☐

5 ひとつのファイルにまとめる

◎グループのメンバーが個別に作成したスライドを同じPC上に並べ、スライドを一枚ずつ「ドラッグ＆ドロップ」、または、「コピー＆ペースト」でひとつのファイルに順番にまとめる。
◎ひとつになったファイルは、メンバー全員が各自のメモリースティックに保存する。

REHEARSE

以下の要領でグループでのリハーサルを行いましょう。

1 原稿を覚える

グループ単位でPCにスライドを写しながら、原稿を覚える。1回目、2回目と回数を重ねるごとに原稿から目を離し、スライドだけをヒントに英語が口をついて出てくるまで練習を繰り返す。

2 相互チェック

グループのメンバー（A, B, C, D）は、Aから順に自分の箇所を発表する。その際、残りのメンバー（B, C, D）は「点検リスト」でAのパフォーマンスをチェックし、コメントする（要領①参照）。次にBが自分の箇所を発表し、残りのメンバーは同様にコメントする（要領②参照）。以下、C, Dについても同じ要領で行う（スマホ等でビデオ撮影をしてもよい）。

要領①

A	自分の箇所を発表
B	Aが話す英語（Speech Message）に焦点をあて、コメントする。
C	Aのスライド（Visual Message）に焦点をあて、コメントする。
D	Aの声、目、手、姿勢（Physical Message）に焦点をあて、コメントする。

要領②

A	Bの声、目、手、姿勢（Physical Message）に焦点をあて、コメントする。
B	自分の箇所を発表
C	Bが話す英語（Speech Message）に焦点をあて、コメントする。
D	Bのスライド（Visual Message）に焦点をあて、コメントする。

点検項目	評価					コメント
❶ SPEECH MESSAGE	1	2	3	4	5	
Plain English	1	2	3	4	5	
Rhetorical Questions	1	2	3	4	5	
Logical	1	2	3	4	5	
Interesting (Funny)	1	2	3	4	5	
❷ VISUAL MESSAGE (Slides)	1	2	3	4	5	
Key Words/Numbers	1	2	3	4	5	
Images (Photos, Illustrations)	1	2	3	4	5	
Charts/Graphs	1	2	3	4	5	
❸ PHYSICAL MESSAGE	1	2	3	4	5	
Voice Inflection	1	2	3	4	5	
Eye Contact	1	2	3	4	5	
Hands (Pointer)	1	2	3	4	5	
Posture	1	2	3	4	5	

3 グループの時間管理（Time Management）

所定の時間内にグループ内のメンバーが全員発表できるように、以下の要領で時間管理をしましょう。

◎下のようなカードを準備してメンバーが交代でTime Keeperを行う。
◎各自の持ち時間の終了15秒前に「15」のカードをプレゼンターに示す。
◎各自の持ち時間が終了したら「NEXT」のカードを示す。
◎「NEXT」のカードが示されたら、即座に次のプレゼンターに替わる。

4 立ち位置

発表時の立ち位置としては一般的に次のような形が考えられます。

HOMEWORK

1. リハーサルの結果、修正の必要があれば修正する。
2. 各自が原稿を見ずにスラスラ言えるようになるまで練習する。
3. グループで発表用の配布資料を準備する（P.24参照）。

WEEK 3 PRESENTATION

プロジェクトの発表を行います。発表の後に自己評価をしましょう。

GIVE A PRESENTATION

- ☐ 配布資料を配る。
- ☐ 原稿を見ずに発表を行う。
- ☐ 制限時間(5分)内にグループ全体を収める。
- ☐ 発表前にスマホ等によるビデオ撮影をクラスメートに依頼する。

EVALUATE YOUR OWN PRESENTATION

撮った映像を見て自己評価をし、次のステップアップにつなげましょう。

評価項目	評価					コメント
❶ SPEECH MESSAGE	1	2	3	4	5	
Plain English	1	2	3	4	5	
Rhetorical Questions	1	2	3	4	5	
Logical	1	2	3	4	5	
Interesting (Funny)	1	2	3	4	5	
❷ VISUAL MESSAGE (Slides)	1	2	3	4	5	
Key Words/Numbers	1	2	3	4	5	
Images (Photos, Illustrations)	1	2	3	4	5	
Charts/Graphs	1	2	3	4	5	
❸ PHYSICAL MESSAGE	1	2	3	4	5	
Voice Inflection	1	2	3	4	5	
Eye Contact	1	2	3	4	5	
Hands (Pointer)	1	2	3	4	5	
Posture	1	2	3	4	5	

特記事項

HOMEWORK

① MISSION 3のサンプル・プレゼンテーションを読む。
② LEARN WORDS, PHRASES & EXPRESSIONS (P.46)に目を通す。
③ 外国人に紹介したい日本の観光スポットを2、3考えてくる。

― MISSION 03 ―
INTRODUCE NICE PLACES IN JAPAN

MISSION 03 では…

外国の人々に日本の訪れて欲しい場所を紹介するプロジェクトです。
定番の観光スポットだけではなく、少し変わった場所などのアイディアを出し合い、
グループで発表しましょう。

CAN-DO LIST

ENGLISH SKILLS

- 外国人に訪れて欲しい日本の場所などについて英語(Sensoji is one of the most...など)で説明できる。
- 文化的、歴史的背景を英語(It was built in...など)で説明することができる。
- 行き方、順路、手順などを英語(Scoop up water and wash your left hand first,...など)で説明できる。

PRESENTATION SKILLS

- 「日本」を説明する印象的なスライドを作成できる。
- 写真やイラストを用いて説明に効果的なスライドを作ることができる。
- 楽しい発表をするための演出がグループでできる。

WEEK 1　PREPARATION 1

プロジェクトの内容と準備の要領を確認し、**WEEK1** の準備を行います。

" MISSION 03 "
INTRODUCE NICE PLACES IN JAPAN

設　定 ▶ 日本の観光スポットを紹介する海外向けテレビ番組
目　的 ▶ 外国の人々に日本のお勧め観光スポットを紹介する。
形　態 ▶ グループ(4人)
時　間 ▶ 5分(グループで)
準　備 ▶ **WEEK 1** … サンプルを読む、語彙・表現を学ぶ、グループで打ち合わせる、原稿を書く。
　　　　WEEK 2 … スライドを作成し、グループで1つにまとめる、リハーサルを行う。
　　　　WEEK 3 … グループで発表する。

LEARN FROM THE SAMPLE Audio 05

SAMPLE

▶ **MC(Chiharu):** Good afternoon, everyone. Today, we're going to introduce you to a nice place in Tokyo. It's Asakusa, which is 20 minutes by train from Tokyo Station. It has many interesting things to see, both new and old. But today, we'd like to take you to an old temple –Sensoji.

▶ We'll tell you about three things you can see and do there: Kaminari-mon, Nakamise, and an incense burner. We'll also explain some of the manners you should observe there. Sho will start.

MISSION 03

Sho: Thank you. Sensoji is one of the most famous tourist spots in Japan. About 30 million people visit it every year. It was built in 628, almost 1,400 years ago, and is the oldest temple in Tokyo. First, let's look at the symbol of Asakusa, Kaminari-mon.

▶ Look at the picture in the center. At the entrance to Sensoji, you see a gate called Kaminari-mon, or "Thunder Gate," with a huge lantern hanging from it. There are two gods protecting the gate. They are Fujin, the God of Wind, and Raijin, the God of Thunder. The official name of the gate is Fujin-Raijin Gate, but it's commonly known as Kaminari-mon.

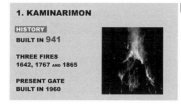

▶ The original Kaminari-mon was built in 941 but it burned down three times in 1642, 1767 and 1865. The present gate was rebuilt in 1960.

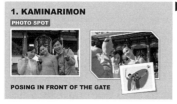

▶ It's one of the most popular sites for taking photos, and is always crowded with tourists, posing in front of the gate.

▶ **MC(Chiharu):** Thanks, Sho. Now, after taking photos at the gate, you go into Sensoji, but before visiting the main hall, there is another thing you can enjoy. Yasuhiro has some information on this.

Yasuhiro: Sure. After you have enjoyed taking photos at the gate, why don't you enjoy shopping next? Go through the gate and you'll see a street called Nakamise-dori. It's Sensoji's shopping street, which stretches about 250 meters. Nakamise-dori opened about 350 years ago. It's one of the oldest shopping streets in Japan with almost 90 shops.

Some sell souvenirs and traditional Japanese items such as kimono, *sensu*, chopsticks, and even ninja goods. They're sure to make nice presents for your families and friends back home.

Other shops sell traditional Japanese snacks such as rice crackers called *senbei*, and steamed cake called *manju*, but probably the most famous one is this – Kaminari-okoshi, a Japanese sweet made from popped rice. As you can probably guess, Kaminari-okoshi was named after Kaminari-mon. This will make a nice present, too.

Some food shops give away free samples out front so that you can try them before you buy.

MC(Chiharu): Sounds nice! Thank you, Yasuhiro. Now, after shopping in Nakamise-dori, it's time to visit the main hall, but there's one thing we recommend you do before that. I'll explain.

3. INCENSE BURNER
INCENSE STICKS / WAVE THE SMOKE FOR GOOD HEALTH

▶ Half way to the main hall, there's an incense burner. First, you buy a bunch of incense sticks, light them and put them in the burner. Then, wave the smoke to the parts of your body that need healing. It's said to have a healing power. The burner is always surrounded by many people. So, you can't miss it.

MC(Chiharu): Now, you're ready to go to the main hall, right?
Mao: Ummm … No, not really. There's just one more thing.
MC(Chiharu): What is it?

OVERVIEW
1. KAMINARIMON
2. NAKAMISE
3. INCENSE BURNER
4. MANNERS AT A TEMPLE

▶ **Mao:** Well, the main hall is a holy place, so you have to purify yourself before you go there. This is part of the basic manners you have to follow at any temple in Japan.

4. MANNERS AT A TEMPLE
PURIFY BEFORE GOING TO THE MAIN HALL
1) WASH YOUR LEFT HAND
2) WASH YOUR RIGHT HAND
3) RINSE YOUR MOUTH

▶ Here, at Sensoji, you'll see a wash-basin near the main hall. Scoop up water and wash your left hand first, and then your right hand. After that, put some water in your left hand and rinse your mouth. Be sure not to put your mouth on the scoop.

4. MANNERS AT THE MAIN HALL
HOW TO PRAY
1) THROW IN COINS
2) PUT HANDS TOGETHER
3) BOW ONCE
4) MAKE A WISH
5) BOW ONE MORE TIME

▶ Next, go up the steps to the main hall. Right in front of the hall, there is a money-box called *saisen-bako*. You throw in some coins, put your hands together, bow once and make a wish. Finally, bow once again.

Is it difficult to remember? Don't worry. If you forget, just look around and do what other people do.

WRAP-UP
1. **KAMINARIMON (SHO)**
   TAKE NICE PHOTOS
2. **NAKAMISE (YASUHIRO)**
   BUY GOOD GIFTS HOME
3. **INCENSE BURNER (CHIHARU)**
   TRY THE HEALING POWER
4. **MANNERS AT A TEMPLE (MAO)**
   LEARN MANNERS

▶ **MC(Chiharu):** Thank you, Mao. So, this is the basic tourist route in Sensoji. Now, let's review what we explained. We first told you about Kaminari-mon Gate. It's a good spot to take photos. Then, Nakamise-dori. Here you can enjoy shopping. After that, try the healing power of incense. Then, you pray. Remember the manners we explained. Well, that's about it for Sensoji.

MANY MORE TO ENJOY
IN & AROUND ASAKUSA

▶ Actually, there are many more things and places you can enjoy in and around Asakusa, like riding a rickshaw or a tour to the Skytree. So, when you visit here, make sure to allow plenty of time for them.

MISSION 03

LEARN WORDS, PHRASES & EXPRESSIONS

プロジェクトに使えそうな語句や表現を学び、原稿作成に活用しましょう。

WORDS & PHRASES

1 観光スポット
sightseeing spot / tourist site / historical place / popular resort / World Heritage Site / national park / theme park / shopping area

2 呼び物
old temple / shrine / castle / national treasure / tower / hot spring / beautiful scenery / local food / local festival / Japanese food restaurant / department store / big discount shop

3 説明
one of the oldest ... / traditional Japanese ... / popular among ... / well known as ... / It's located in ... / in western Japan / three hours by *Shinkansen* from Tokyo / ... is 20 minutes by train from ...

4 その他
capsule hotel / *ryokan* / *izakaya* or Japanese style pub / *kaiten-zushi* restaurant / *karaoke*

EXPRESSIONS

1 「観光スポットを紹介する」
We'd like to introduce you to ... / Why don't you visit ...? / Make sure to visit ... / It's famous for ...

2 「見ること・経験することを勧める」
We recommend you see... / You can see ... / You can enjoy ... / You can experience ...

PRESENTATION TECHNIQUES
" 言葉と手で注目させる "

SAMPLE の第4ブロック Look at the picture in the center....There are two gods protecting the gate. They are Fujin, the God of Wind, and Raijin, the God of Thunder.	スライドはただ映しているだけでは十分な効果を得られません。プレゼンターは要所で手(ポインター)を使い、スライド上の写真やキーワードを指し示す必要があります。Look at the picture... のような言葉も加えると、聴衆の注目を確実に得られます。

DECIDE WHAT YOU TALK ABOUT

サンプル・プレゼンテーションを参考に、以下の要領で内容を決めましょう。

1 リーダー（グループのまとめ役）とMC（司会進行役）を決める。
2 MCは進行役に加え、自分のPOINTも担当する。
3 グループで協議し、自然な論旨が展開できるよう各自のPOINTを決める。
4 決まった内容を下の表に記入し、グループで共有する。

【サンプル・プレゼンテーション】

	内容	担当	時間
INTRODUCTION	Greeting / Overview	MC	0'15"
POINT 1	Kaminarimon	将	1'00"
	transition	MC	0'10"
POINT 2	Nakamise	靖弘	1'00"
	transition	MC	0'10"
POINT 3	Incense Burner	千春	1'00"
	transition	MC	0'10"
POINT 4	Manners at a Temple	真央	1'00"
CONCLUSION	Wrap-Up / Greeting	MC	0'15"

【あなたのグループのプレゼンテーション】

	内容	担当	時間
INTRODUCTION	Greeting / Overview	MC	0'15"
POINT 1			1'00"
	transition	MC	0'10"
POINT 2			1'00"
	transition	MC	0'10"
POINT 3			1'00"
	transition	MC	0'10"
POINT 4			1'00"
CONCLUSION	Wrap-Up / Greeting	MC	0'15"

PREPARE YOUR SPEECH MESSAGE

【あなたのグループのプレゼンテーション】を元に、原稿を作成しましょう（パソコンのWordに直接書き込んでも可）。

MISSION 03

❶ 主要な英文を作成しましょう。

▼「紹介したい観光スポット」について：
　Today, we're going to introduce you to ... などを使って

```
[                                                                    ]
```

▼「見て欲しいもの」について：
　We recommend you see... / You can see ... などを使って

```
[                                                                    ]
```

▼「経験して欲しいこと」について：
　Why don't you ... / You can enjoy ... などを使って

```
[                                                                    ]
```

❷ 作成した主要な英文を中心に枝葉をつけて、自分の担当箇所の原稿（150語前後）を完成させましょう。

❸ 原稿の点検

作成した原稿（Speech Message）を「点検リスト」でチェックしましょう。

SPEECH MESSAGE の点検	点検のポイント	チェック
① Number of Words	時間に対して語数は適量か	☐
② Plain English	平易な英語で書かれているか	☐
③ Rhetorical Questions	聴衆への問い掛けはあるか	☐
④ Logical	論理的に書かれているか	☐
⑤ Interesting (Funny)	興味深い内容になっているか	☐

❹ MC担当者は進行のための原稿も準備しましょう。

◎【あなたのグループのプレゼンテーション】を元に、
　グループ全体のINTRODUCTIONとCONCLUSIONの原稿を準備する。
◎【あなたのグループのプレゼンテーション】を元に、プレゼンターとプレゼンターの橋渡し
　（transition）の原稿も準備する（P.32のPRESENTATION TECHNIQUESを参照）。

HOMEWORK

① 原稿が未完成の場合は完成させ、点検する。
② 次回のスライド作成のための材料（写真、イラストなど）を準備する。

WEEK 2　PREPARATION 2

WEEK2 の準備をします。スライドを作成し、リハーサルを行います。

PREPARE YOUR VISUAL MESSAGE

❶ スライドの構成と内容 ➡ （P.35を参照）

❷ スライドの作成 ➡ （P.35を参照）

❸ 今回のプロジェクトでの工夫：日本語を英語でフォローする
　スライドに日本語が使われる場合は、必ず英語で説明を加えましょう（下の例を参照）。

 Scoop up water and wash your left hand first, (中略), put some water in your left hand and rinse your mouth.

❹ スライドの点検
　作成したスライド（Visual Message）を「点検リスト」でチェックしましょう。

VISUAL MESSAGE の点検	点検のポイント	チェック
① Number of Slides	スライドの枚数は適当か	☐
② Key Words/Numbers	重要な語句や数字は書かれているか	☐
③ Images (Photos, Illustrations)	写真やイラストは効果的に使えているか	☐
④ Charts/Graphs	図表やグラフは効果的に使えているか	☐

❺ ひとつのファイルにまとめる ➡ （P.36を参照）

REHEARSE

以下の要領でグループでのリハーサルを行いましょう。

❶ 原稿を覚える
　グループ単位でPCにスライドを写しながら、原稿を覚える。1回目、2回目と回数を重ねるごとに原稿から目を離し、スライドだけをヒントに英語が口をついて出てくるまで練習を繰り返す。

❷ 相互チェック ➡ （P.36を参照）

MISSION 03

点検項目	評価					コメント
❶ SPEECH MESSAGE	1	2	3	4	5	
Plain English	1	2	3	4	5	
Rhetorical Questions	1	2	3	4	5	
Logical	1	2	3	4	5	
Interesting (Funny)	1	2	3	4	5	
❷ VISUAL MESSAGE (Slides)	1	2	3	4	5	
Key Words/Numbers	1	2	3	4	5	
Images (Photos, Illustrations)	1	2	3	4	5	
Charts/Graphs	1	2	3	4	5	
❸ PHYSICAL MESSAGE	1	2	3	4	5	
Voice Inflection	1	2	3	4	5	
Eye Contact	1	2	3	4	5	
Hands (Pointer)	1	2	3	4	5	
Posture	1	2	3	4	5	

❸ グループの時間管理（Time Management）
所定の時間内にグループ内のメンバーが全員発表できるように、時間管理をしましょう。
➡ （P.37を参照）

❹ 立ち位置 ➡ （P.38を参照）

HOMEWORK
① リハーサルの結果、修正の必要があれば修正する。
② 各自が原稿を見ずにスラスラ言えるようになるまで練習する。
③ グループで発表用の配布資料を準備する（P.24参照）。

WEEK 3 PRESENTATION

プロジェクトの発表を行います。発表の後に自己評価をしましょう。

GIVE A PRESENTATION

☐ 配布資料を配る。
☐ 原稿を見ずに発表を行う。
☐ 制限時間(5分)内にグループ全体を収める。
☐ 発表前にスマホ等によるビデオ撮影をクラスメートに依頼する。

EVALUATE YOUR OWN PRESENTATION

撮った映像を見て自己評価をし、次のステップアップにつなげましょう。

評価項目	評価					コメント
❶ SPEECH MESSAGE	1	2	3	4	5	
Plain English	1	2	3	4	5	
Rhetorical Questions	1	2	3	4	5	
Logical	1	2	3	4	5	
Interesting (Funny)	1	2	3	4	5	
❷ VISUAL MESSAGE (Slides)	1	2	3	4	5	
Key Words/Numbers	1	2	3	4	5	
Images (Photos, Illustrations)	1	2	3	4	5	
Charts/Graphs	1	2	3	4	5	
❸ PHYSICAL MESSAGE	1	2	3	4	5	
Voice Inflection	1	2	3	4	5	
Eye Contact	1	2	3	4	5	
Hands (Pointer)	1	2	3	4	5	
Posture	1	2	3	4	5	

特記事項

HOMEWORK

① MISSION 4のサンプル・プレゼンテーションを読む。
② LEARN WORDS, PHRASES & EXPRESSIONS (P.57)に目を通す。
③ 自分の夏休みの計画について2、3考えてくる。

― MISSION 04 ―
TALK ABOUT YOUR SUMMER PLANS

MISSION 04 では…

あなたの夏休みの予定や計画をクラスメートに伝える個人のプロジェクトです。
すでに予定していることや計画していること、あるいは、
やってみたいと考えていることなどを具体的にわかりやすく伝えましょう。

CAN-DO LIST

ENGLISH SKILLS

- 個人の予定、計画、希望について英語で原稿を準備し、発表することができる。
- 「予定・計画」の表現（I'm going to … など）が適切にできる。
- 「希望・願望」の表現（I'd like to … など）が適切にできる。

PRESENTATION SKILLS

- 予定・計画の「情報伝達」が効果的にできる。
- 写真、イラスト、フローチャート（「矢印」）を効果的に使うことができる。
- アニメーション機能を効果的に使うことができる。

WEEK 1　PREPARATION 1

プロジェクトの内容と準備の要領を確認し、**WEEK1** の準備を行います。

" MISSION 04 "
TALK ABOUT YOUR SUMMER PLANS

設 定 ▶ 留学生が在籍するクラス
目 的 ▶ 自分の夏休みの計画を立て、クラスの前で発表することにより、計画的な充実した夏休みが過ごせるようにする。
形 態 ▶ 個人
時 間 ▶ 1分（2分＊）　＊余裕のあるクラスは発表を2分間にし、3週間で準備し、WEEK4で「発表」としてもよい。
準 備 ▶ **WEEK 1** … サンプルを読む、語彙・表現を学ぶ、原稿を書く。
　　　　WEEK 2 … スライドを作成し、リハーサルを行う。
　　　　WEEK 3 … 発表する。

LEARN FROM THE SAMPLES

SAMPLE 1　Audio 06

▶ Hi, everyone. I'm Katsuya Okada. What are you planning for this summer? I'm going to take a trip to Hokkaido.

▶ Before I go, I'll work part-time. I'm working at a convenience store now. But during the summer, I'll take one more job as a lifeguard at a swimming pool.

▶ Then, with the money I make from my part-time jobs, I'll go to Hokkaido with some friends. They're good old friends from junior high school.

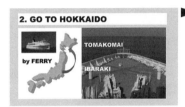

▶ We'll take a ferry from Ibaraki to Tomakomai, and then …

▶ we'll drive around in Hokkaido for a week. I got a driver's license last summer.

▶ To save money and make the trip more exciting and memorable, we'll camp as we go from place to place throughout the trip. Oh, no! No bears, please! It's too exciting!

▶ These are my plans for this summer. I'll work hard and play hard. Thank you.

SAMPLE 2 🔊 Audio 07

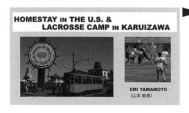

▶ Hello, everyone. I'm Emi Yamamoto.

▶ This summer, I'm going on a homestay in San Francisco in August for 3 weeks. It's a little scary because this is my first trip overseas and I'm not really confident about my English.

▶ I hear people from many Asian countries come to the school I'm going to attend. So, I hope to make friends with them.

▶ Spending time with my host family is another thing I'm looking forward to. These will be good chances for me to learn about different cultures.

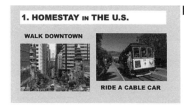

▶ Also, in San Francisco, I want to walk around downtown and ride a cable car.

► After coming back to Japan, I'm going to join a 4-day camp with my lacrosse club members. We'll go to Karuizawa. We'll not only practice lacrosse but have fun, too. We plan to have a BBQ and enjoy fireworks.

► I can't wait for the summer vacation! Thank you.

LEARN WORDS, PHRASES & EXPRESSIONS

プロジェクトに使えそうな語句や表現を学び、原稿作成に活用しましょう。

WORDS & PHRASES

1 旅行
go to ... with friends from junior high school / go on a homestay in ... / take a trip to ... with my family / go camping in ...

2 アルバイト
work part-time at ... / have a part time job / help my family business / save money by working part time / work at a *juku* school during the summer

3 合宿
have a training camp / join a 4-day camp with ... / hard but fun, too / go to ... for a seminar camp / have a party / get closer to juniors and seniors

4 帰省
go back to my home in ... / spend time with my family / see my old friends from elementary school / have a class reunion / enjoy the local summer festival

5 その他
enjoy a BBQ / get a driver's license / go to driving school / go and enjoy a firework display / take a summer intensive course of English / study for the TOEIC® test

EXPRESSIONS

1 「予定・計画」
I'm going to ... / I plan to ... / I think I will ... / I'm thinking of ~ ing ...

2 「希望・願望」
I'd like to ... / I want to .... / I hope to ...

3 「期待」
I'm looking forward to ... / I'm really excited. / I can't wait for ...!

PRESENTATION TECHNIQUES
" 聴衆に問い掛ける "

SAMPLE 1の第1ブロック Hi, everyone. I'm Katsuya Okada. **What are you planning for this summer?** I'm going to take a trip to Hokkaido.	プレゼンターが始終一方的に話したのでは聴衆の注意を引きつけ維持することはできません。What are you planning ...? のように要所要所で聴衆に問い掛けましょう。問い掛けた後、短いポーズ(2秒)を取ります。

DECIDE WHAT YOU TALK ABOUT

サンプル・プレゼンテーションを参考にブレーンストーミングを行い、あなた自身のプレゼンテーションの内容を決めましょう。(下の【あなたのプレゼンテーション】にメモ)。

【SAMPLE1のプレゼンテーション】

タイトル	アルバイト、北海道旅行
Point 1 アルバイト	今：コンビニ 夏：もうひとつ プールの監視員
Point 2 旅　行	貯めたお金で北海道 中学時代の友人と フェリーで：茨城→苫小牧 車で回る １週間 キャンプ：節約、面白い

【あなたのプレゼンテーション】

PREPARE YOUR SPEECH MESSAGE

【あなたのプレゼンテーション】を元に、原稿を作成しましょう（パソコンのWordに直接書き込んでも可）。

1 主要な英文を作成しましょう。

▼「予定・計画」について：
　I'm going to ... / I plan to ... などを使って

▼「希望・願望」について：
　I'd like to ... / I want to ... などを使って

▼「期待」について：
　I'm looking forward to ... などを使って

2 作成した主要な英文を中心に枝葉をつけて、INTRODUCTION, BODY, CONCLUSIONの構成を整えて、原稿全体（150語前後）を完成させましょう。

3 原稿の点検

作成した原稿（Speech Message）を「点検リスト」でチェックしましょう。

SPEECH MESSAGEの点検	点検のポイント	チェック
① Number of Words	時間に対して語数は適量か	☐
② Plain English	平易な英語で書かれているか	☐
③ Rhetorical Questions	聴衆への問い掛けはあるか	☐
④ Logical	論理的に書かれているか	☐
⑤ Interesting (Funny)	興味深い内容になっているか	☐

HOMEWORK

① 原稿が未完成の場合は完成させ、点検する。
② 次回のスライド作成のための材料（写真、イラストなど）を準備する。

WEEK 2 PREPARATION 2

WEEK2の準備をします。スライドを作成し、リハーサルを行います。

PREPARE YOUR VISUAL MESSAGE

1 スライドの作成

サンプル・プレゼンテーションのスライドを参考に、あなた自身のスライドを原稿と照らし合わせながら作成しましょう。

【SAMPLE1のスライドの構成と内容】

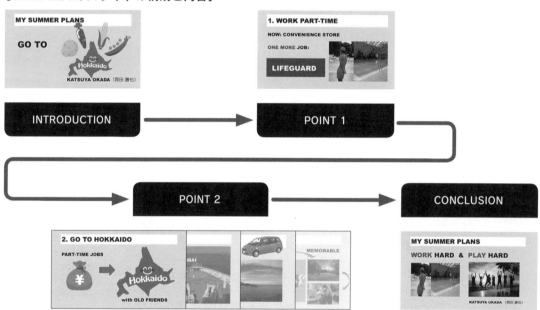

2 今回のプロジェクトでの工夫：「矢印」を使う。

時間的・物理的な移動や因果関係などを示すために、「矢印」を効果的につかいましょう。
ツールバーから[挿入]➡[図形]でいろいろな「矢印」が見つかります。

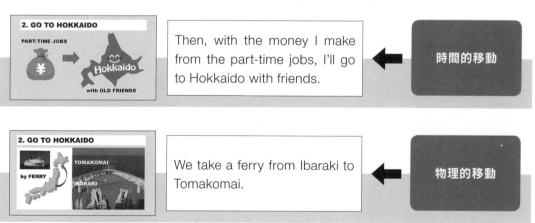

3 スライドの点検

作成したスライド(Visual Message)を「点検リスト」でチェックしましょう。

VISUAL MESSAGE の点検	点検のポイント	チェック
① Number of Slides	スライドの枚数は適当か	☐
② Key Words/Numbers	重要な語句や数字は書かれているか	☐
③ Images (Photos, Illustrations)	写真やイラストは効果的に使えているか	☐
④ Charts/Graphs	図表やグラフは効果的に使えているか	☐

REHEARSE

以下の要領でリハーサルをしましょう。

1 原稿を覚える

自分のPCでスライドを見ながら(ツールバーで[スライドショー])原稿を覚える。1回目、2回目と回数を重ねるごとに原稿から目を離し、スライドだけをヒントに英語が口をついて出てくるまで練習を繰り返す。

2 ペア練習 (A:プレゼンター、B:聞き手)

ペアを組んで各自3回リハーサルを行う。プレゼンターは自分のPCでスライドを見せながら発表し、聞き手は「点検リスト」でプレゼンターのパフォーマンスをチェックする(スマホ等でビデオ撮影をしてもよい)。

	A	B
1回目	発 表	Aが話す英語(Speech Message)に焦点をあてコメントする。
2回目	発 表	スライド(Visual Message)に焦点をあてコメントする。
3回目	発 表	声、目、手、姿勢(Physical Message)に焦点をあてコメントする。

引き続きAとBは役割を換え、同様の練習を行う。

点 検 項 目	評 価					コ メ ン ト
1 SPEECH MESSAGE	1	2	3	4	5	
Plain English	1	2	3	4	5	
Rhetorical Questions	1	2	3	4	5	
Logical	1	2	3	4	5	
Interesting (Funny)	1	2	3	4	5	
2 VISUAL MESSAGE (Slides)	1	2	3	4	5	
Key Words/Numbers	1	2	3	4	5	
Images (Photos, Illustrations)	1	2	3	4	5	
Charts/Graphs	1	2	3	4	5	
3 PHYSICAL MESSAGE	1	2	3	4	5	
Voice Inflection	1	2	3	4	5	
Eye Contact	1	2	3	4	5	
Hands (Pointer)	1	2	3	4	5	
Posture	1	2	3	4	5	

HOMEWORK

1. リハーサルの結果、修正の必要があれば修正する。
2. 原稿を見ずにスラスラ言えるようになるまで練習する。
3. 発表用の配布資料を準備する（P.24参照）。

TALK ABOUT YOUR SUMMER PLANS

WEEK 3 PRESENTATION

プロジェクトの発表を行います。発表の後に自己評価をしましょう。

GIVE A PRESENTATION

☐ 配付資料を配る。
☐ 原稿を見ずに発表を行う。
☐ 制限時間（1分）内に全体を収める。
☐ 発表前にスマホ等によるビデオ撮影をクラスメートに依頼する。

EVALUATE YOUR OWN PRESENTATION

撮った映像を見て自己評価をし、次のステップアップにつなげましょう。

評価項目	評 価					コメント
❶ SPEECH MESSAGE	1	2	3	4	5	
Plain English	1	2	3	4	5	
Rhetorical Questions	1	2	3	4	5	
Logical	1	2	3	4	5	
Interesting (Funny)	1	2	3	4	5	
❷ VISUAL MESSAGE (Slides)	1	2	3	4	5	
Key Words/Numbers	1	2	3	4	5	
Images (Photos, Illustrations)	1	2	3	4	5	
Charts/Graphs	1	2	3	4	5	
❸ PHYSICAL MESSAGE	1	2	3	4	5	
Voice Inflection	1	2	3	4	5	
Eye Contact	1	2	3	4	5	
Hands (Pointer)	1	2	3	4	5	
Posture	1	2	3	4	5	

特記事項

HOMEWORK

① MISSION 5のサンプル・プレゼンテーションを読む。
② LEARN WORDS, PHRASES & EXPRESSIONS（P.69）に目を通す。

MISSION 05
INTRODUCE YOUR CLASSMATES

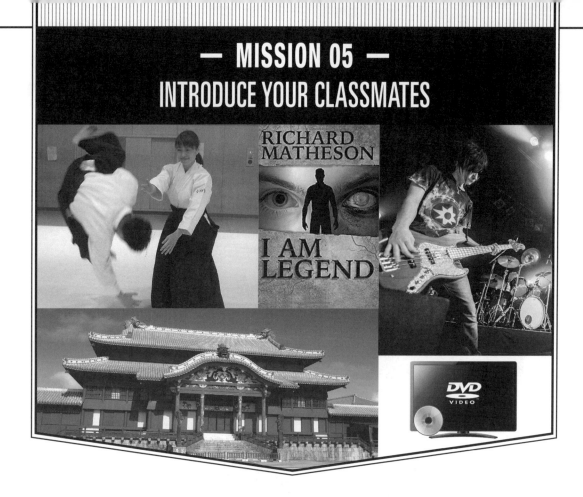

MISSION 05 では…

自己紹介ではなく、あなたのクラスメートを紹介します。

クラスメートの一人について調べ、自分の印象や相手から聞き取ったことなどを整理し、わかりやすく伝えましょう。

CAN-DO LIST

ENGLISH SKILLS

- 「人物の説明」について英語で原稿を準備し、口頭で発表することができる。
- 「紹介」の表現 (Let me introduce … など) が適切にできる。
- 「人物描写」の表現 (She's active and energetic …など) が適切にできる。

PRESENTATION SKILLS

- 個人でプロジェクトの準備、および実施ができる。
- 取材し、情報を整理し、それを効果的に伝達することができる。
- 写真、イラスト、フローチャートを効果的に使うことができる。

WEEK 1　PREPARATION 1

プロジェクトの内容と準備の要領を確認し、**WEEK1** の準備を行います。

" MISSION 05 "
INTRODUCE YOUR CLASSMATES

設　定 ▶ 留学生が在籍するクラスの学期初め
目　的 ▶ クラスメートの1人をクラス全体に紹介し、その人物についてよく理解し、知ってもらう。
形　態 ▶ 個人
時　間 ▶ 1分
準　備 ▶ **WEEK 1** … サンプルを読む、語彙・表現を学ぶ、原稿を書く。
　　　　WEEK 2 … スライドを作成し、リハーサルを行う。
　　　　WEEK 3 … 発表する。

LEARN FROM THE SAMPLES

SAMPLE 1　　Audio 08

▶ Good afternoon, everyone. I'm Eita Yamashita and here's my classmate, Ayaka Inoue. Let me introduce her.

▶ Ayaka is a first-year student, majoring in law. She comes from Sendai. My first impression of her was that she was a quiet and passive type of girl. But actually she is not.

MISSION 05

► Ayaka is an active and energetic athlete. She practices aikido in the university club. And, to my surprise, she has a black belt! So, be careful. If you touch her, she'll kill you!

► Besides aikido, Ayaka likes watching movies on DVDs. Almost every weekend, she watches one or two movies. She really is a big movie fan.

► She loves Disney movies like many other girls, and she also likes the Harry Potter series, Ghibli animations and many others.

► Ayaka likes English, but she says she is not really good at it. So, will you please help her?

► Me? Of course, I will. Otherwise, she'll kill me. Thank you.

SAMPLE 2 Audio 09

▶ Hi, I'm Akane. I'd like to introduce Makoto Kobayashi.

▶ He is a second-year student and majors in Economics. According to him, he's taking this class again because he failed it last year.

▶ Makoto was born and raised in Okinawa, near Shurijo Castle. It's one of the most popular sightseeing spots.

▶ He learned to play *sanshin*, a traditional Okinawa string instrument, when he was a child.

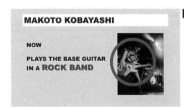

▶ Now he plays the base guitar in a rock band. Wow, what a difference!

MISSION 05

► He likes reading and his room is full of books. Science fiction is his favorite genre. He especially loves Richard Matheson. Does anyone know him? No ... nobody. Oh, sorry. I don't know him, either.

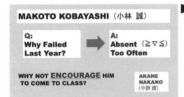

► By the way, I asked Makoto why he failed this class last year. He said he was absent too often. So, why don't we encourage him to come to class and help him succeed this year? Thank you.

LEARN WORDS, PHRASES & EXPRESSIONS

プロジェクトに使えそうな語句や表現を学び、原稿作成に活用しましょう。

WORDS & PHRASES

1 学年、専攻 (MISSION01, WORDS&PHRASES参照)
failed last semester / take this course again / repeater / get credit / new student

2 性格、性質 (MISSION01, WORDS&PHRASES参照)
quiet and passive type of girl / active / energetic / kind / friendly / outgoing / charming / talkative / bossy / faithful / sympathetic / easygoing / stubborn

3 趣味、特技 (MISSION01, WORDS&PHRASES参照)
go window-shopping / play video games / hang out with friends / do photography / cooking

EXPRESSIONS

1「紹介」
Let me introduce ... / I'd like to introduce ... / Here's ... / This is ...

2「趣味、特技」
like to ... / (do) ... in one's spare time / be a big soccer fan / be good at ... / be excellent in ...

3「苦手」
don't like ... / be not really good at ... / can't (do) ... well / not a good cook

4「情報源」
She says (that) ... / According to him, ... / She thinks (that) ...

5「印象」
My first impression of her is ... / I thought he was ... but in fact he is ... / She looks ...

PRESENTATION TECHNIQUES
" ジョークで和ませる "

SAMPLE 1の第3ブロック
…, she has a black belt! So, be careful. If you touch her, she'll kill you!

SAMPLE 1の第6, 7ブロック
So, will you please help her? Me? Of course, I will. Otherwise, she'll kill me.

▶ ジョークを入れるとプレゼンテーションが和みます。ポイントは、①シンプルに、②スライドと絡める、です。「すべらない」ためには、ジョークを言った後に "It's a joke." と言って自分が率先して笑うことです。

DECIDE WHAT YOU TALK ABOUT

サンプル・プレゼンテーションを参考に、あなた自身のプレゼンテーションの内容を決めます。事前に紹介する相手を決め、取材をしましょう。(下の【あなたのプレゼンテーション】にメモ)。

【SAMPLE1のプレゼンテーション】

タイトル	クラスメート 井上綾香
Point 1 背　景	1年生 法学部
Point 2 性　格 特　技	第一印象：静か、消極的 実は：活発、アスリート 合気道、黒帯
Point 3 趣　味	DVDで映画 毎週1，2本 ディズニー、ハリーポッター、ジブリ
Point 4 苦　手	英語：好きだけど苦手 助けてやろう

【あなたのプレゼンテーション】

PREPARE YOUR SPEECH MESSAGE

【あなたのプレゼンテーション】を元に、原稿を作成しましょう（パソコンのWordに直接書き込んでも可）。

1 主要な英文を作成しましょう。

▼「趣味・特技」について：
　He likes to ... / She is excellent in ... などを使って

INTRODUCE YOUR CLASSMATES

▼「苦手」について：
　He doesn't like ... / She is not good at ... などを使って

▼「印象」について：
　My first impression of her is ... / She looks ... などを使って

2 作成した主要な英文を中心に枝葉をつけて、INTRODUCTION, BODY, CONCLUSIONの構成を整えて、原稿全体(150語前後)を完成させましょう。

3 原稿の点検

作成した原稿(Speech Message)を「点検リスト」でチェックしましょう。

SPEECH MESSAGEの点検	点検のポイント	チェック
① Number of Words	時間に対して語数は適量か	☐
② Plain English	平易な英語で書かれているか	☐
③ Rhetorical Questions	聴衆への問い掛けはあるか	☐
④ Logical	論理的に書かれているか	☐
⑤ Interesting (Funny)	興味深い内容になっているか ジョークは入っているか	☐

HOMEWORK

① 原稿が未完成の場合は完成させ、点検する。
② 次回のスライド作成のための材料(写真、イラストなど)を準備する。

WEEK 2　PREPARATION 2

WEEK 2の準備をします。スライドを作成し、リハーサルを行います。

PREPARE YOUR VISUAL MESSAGE

1 スライドの作成

サンプル・プレゼンテーションのスライドを参考に、あなた自身のスライドを原稿と照らし合わせながら作成しましょう。

【SAMPLE1のスライドの構成と内容】

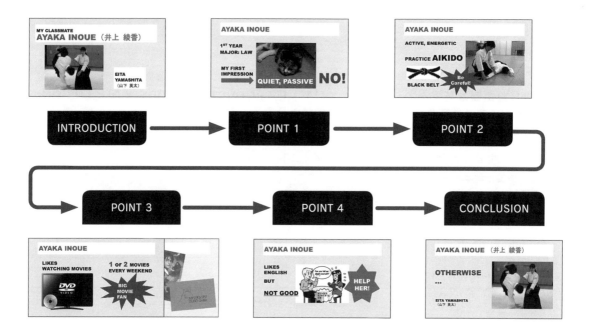

2 今回のプロジェクトでの工夫：「図形」で強調する。

驚きを表現したり、強く訴えたりするようなときには「図形」を効果的につかいましょう。
ツールバーから[挿入] ➡ [図形]でいろいろな「図形」が見つかります。
「図形」の中には文字を書き込むことができます。

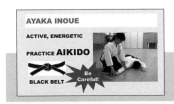 And, to my surprise, she has a black belt! So, **be careful**. ←

 ... she says she is not really good at it. So, will you please **help her**? ←

3 スライドの点検

作成したスライド（Visual Message）を「点検リスト」でチェックしましょう。

VISUAL MESSAGEの点検	点検のポイント	チェック
① Number of Slides	スライドの枚数は適当か	☐
② Key Words/Numbers	重要な語句や数字は書かれているか	☐
③ Images (Photos, Illustrations)	写真やイラストは効果的に使えているか	☐
④ Charts / Graphs	図表やグラフは効果的に使えているか	☐

REHEARSE

以下の要領でリハーサルをしましょう。

1 原稿を覚える

自分のPCでスライドを見ながら（ツールバーで[スライドショー]）原稿を覚える。1回目、2回目と回数を重ねるごとに原稿から目を離し、スライドだけをヒントに英語が口をついて出てくるまで練習を繰り返す。

2 ペア練習 （A：プレゼンター、B：聞き手）

ペアを組んで各自3回リハーサルを行う。プレゼンターは自分のPCでスライドを見せながら発表し、聞き手は「点検リスト」でプレゼンターのパフォーマンスをチェックする（スマホ等でビデオ撮影をしてもよい）。

	A	B
1回目	発 表	Aが話す英語（Speech Message）に焦点をあてコメントする。
2回目	発 表	スライド（Visual Message）に焦点をあてコメントする。
3回目	発 表	声、目、手、姿勢（Physical Message）に焦点をあてコメントする。

引き続きAとBは役割を換え、同様の練習を行う。

点検項目	評　価					コメント
❶ SPEECH MESSAGE	1	2	3	4	5	
Plain English	1	2	3	4	5	
Rhetorical Questions	1	2	3	4	5	
Logical	1	2	3	4	5	
Interesting (Funny)	1	2	3	4	5	
❷ VISUAL MESSAGE (Slides)	1	2	3	4	5	
Key Words/Numbers	1	2	3	4	5	
Images (Photos, Illustrations)	1	2	3	4	5	
Charts/Graphs	1	2	3	4	5	
❸ PHYSICAL MESSAGE	1	2	3	4	5	
Voice Inflection	1	2	3	4	5	
Eye Contact	1	2	3	4	5	
Hands (Pointer)	1	2	3	4	5	
Posture	1	2	3	4	5	

HOMEWORK

① リハーサルの結果、修正の必要があれば修正する。
② 原稿を見ずにスラスラ言えるようになるまで練習する。
③ 発表用の配布資料を準備する（P.24参照）。

INTRODUCE YOUR CLASSMATES

WEEK 3 PRESENTATION

プロジェクトの発表を行います。発表の後に自己評価をしましょう。

GIVE A PRESENTATION

☐ 配付資料を配る。
☐ 原稿を見ずに発表を行う。
☐ 制限時間（1分）内に全体を収める。
☐ 発表前にスマホ等によるビデオ撮影をクラスメートに依頼する。

EVALUATE YOUR OWN PRESENTATION

撮った映像を見て自己評価をし、次のステップアップにつなげましょう。

評価項目	評　価					コメント
1 SPEECH MESSAGE	1	2	3	4	5	
Plain English	1	2	3	4	5	
Rhetorical Questions	1	2	3	4	5	
Logical	1	2	3	4	5	
Interesting (Funny)	1	2	3	4	5	
2 VISUAL MESSAGE (Slides)	1	2	3	4	5	
Key Words/Numbers	1	2	3	4	5	
Images (Photos, Illustrations)	1	2	3	4	5	
Charts/Graphs	1	2	3	4	5	
3 PHYSICAL MESSAGE	1	2	3	4	5	
Voice Inflection	1	2	3	4	5	
Eye Contact	1	2	3	4	5	
Hands (Pointer)	1	2	3	4	5	
Posture	1	2	3	4	5	

特記事項

HOMEWORK

① MISSION 6のサンプル・プレゼンテーションを読む。
② LEARN WORDS, PHRASES & EXPRESSIONS（P.82）に目を通す。
③ 外国人に紹介したい日本の文化（行事、習慣など）を2、3考えてくる。

— MISSION 06 —
EXPLAIN JAPANESE CULTURE

MISSION 06 では…

外国の人々に日本の文化や習慣を紹介するグループ・プロジェクトです。

皆さんが伝えたいと思うテーマを選び、

それを平易な語句や表現でわかりやすく説明しましょう。

CAN-DO LIST

ENGLISH SKILLS

- 日本の文化について英語で原稿を準備し、口頭で発表することができる。
- 日本独特のものについて英語(*kadomatsu*, a pair of pine decorationsなど)で説明、表現することができる。
- 複雑な概念を英語(For example, …など)でわかりやすく説明することができる。

PRESENTATION SKILLS

- 日本独特のものを写真やイラストで示すことができる。
- チャートを使って情報を整理することができる。
- グループ発表の時間管理ができる。

WEEK 1　PREPARATION 1

プロジェクトの内容と準備の要領を確認し、**WEEK1** の準備を行います。

" MISSION 06 "
EXPLAIN JAPANESE CULTURE

設 定 ▶ 「日本の文化、習慣」を紹介する海外向けテレビ番組
目 的 ▶ 海外の人々に日本の文化や習慣について理解を深めてもらう。
形 態 ▶ グループ（4人）
時 間 ▶ 5分（グループで）
準 備 ▶ **WEEK 1** … サンプルを読む、語彙・表現を学ぶ、グループで打ち合わせる、原稿を書く。
　　　　WEEK 2 … スライドを作成し、グループで1つにまとめる、リハーサルを行う。
　　　　WEEK 3 … グループで発表する。

LEARN FROM THE SAMPLE　　　　🔊 Audio 10

SAMPLE

▶ **MC(Ryoji):** Good afternoon, everyone. We are Group 7, and I'm Ryoji Kawamura, leader of the group.

▶ Every country has annual events that are related to their religions. It's the same here in Japan. In our presentation today, we'll focus on winter events. We'll talk about how we spend 1) Christmas, 2) the year-end, 3) the New Year's holiday, and 4) our unique ideas about religions. So. Let's begin with Christmas. Emi.

▶ **Emi:** All right, Ryoji. Although the major religions in Japan are Shinto and Buddhism, many people celebrate Christmas.

MISSION 06

▶ As in Western countries, a lot of shops and stores here start Christmas sales in November. They sell Christmas-related items and goods for Christmas presents. In December, cake shops also get very busy, especially on Christmas Eve, with people getting special Christmas cakes.

▶ Shops and streets are decorated with colorful illuminations, and Christmas songs are heard everywhere. The whole town is in a Christmas mood.

▶ On Christmas Eve or Christmas Day, people have a party. Some celebrate it at home with their families. Others go out to restaurants. Parents give their children presents, and couples exchange them. For most Japanese, Christmas is not a religious event. It's just a fun time for families, couples, and friends.

MC(Ryoji): Thanks, Emi. Now, once Christmas ends, the New Year mood begins to fill the country. Takeshi will tell you about it.

▶ **Takeshi:** The winter holiday in Japan typically starts on December 29th and lasts until January 3rd. Preparations for New Year's usually begins around the time the winter holiday starts. Families prepare *osechi-ryori*, or traditional New Year's dishes.

▶ Also, they set up *kadomatsu*, a pair of pine decorations, in front of the gates. This is to welcome gods to their homes.

▶ On New Year's Eve, people eat *toshikoshi-soba* or year-crossing noodles, wishing for a long life.

▶ And people enjoy a TV show called *Kohaku-Utagassen*, a singing competition between male and female singers. It's a traditional way many Japanese like to spend the evening.

▶ Then at midnight, people listen to *joyano-kane*, or striking of a bell, from nearby temples. *Joyano-kane* is struck 108 times because in Buddhism, it's believed that humans have 108 bad desires and the bells remove them all.

MC(Ryoji): Thanks, Takeshi. Now, you know how we spend the year end in Japan, but how about New Year's Day? I'll explain.

▶ **Ryoji:** For breakfast on New Year's Day, we have a special menu.

▶ We eat *osechi-ryori*. It consists of many kinds of dishes as you see here: lobsters, fish cake, rolled omelette, herring roe, black soybeans, and so on. Each dish has some lucky meaning. They are beautiful to look at, and delicious to eat.

▶ Another common practice is *otoshidama*, or gift money given to children by their parents. For many children, this is their happiest moment during the New Year's holiday.

▶ Just as people in Western countries go to churches during Christmas, Japanese people visit shrines during the New Year's holiday. It's called *hatsumode*, or the first visit to a shrine.

▶ People throw money into *saisen-bako*, or an offering box, placed in front of a shrine and pray for happiness and good luck. Some people also buy *omikuji*, a fortune-telling paper, which tells you your fortune for the year.

▶ At shrines during the holiday, you can see some women dressed in beautiful traditional kimono. Well, that's about the New Year's holiday.

MC(Ryoji): Now, let's take a look at what we have mentioned again and see how it is related to religions. Karen will talk about it.

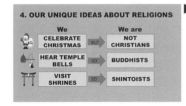

▶ **Karen:** We celebrate Christmas but we're not Christians. When we hear temple bells on New Year's Eve, we're Buddhists. And when we visit shrines for *hatsumode*, we're Shintoists. Why is that? It's because we don't have a strong faith in a particular religion. In fact, we seldom go to temples or shrines, except for some special occasions.

▶ But this doesn't necessarily mean Japanese have little religious belief. In Buddhism, we believe we'll all become a Buddha when we die. So we respect every other person.

▶ And in Shintoism, we believe that gods exist in everything and everywhere like in the trees and in the mountains. So we pay respect to everything around us. All these may sound strange to you, but these are our unique ideas about religions.

▶ **MC(Ryoji):** Thank you, Karen. Today, we talked about how we spend Christmas, year-end and the New Year's holiday in Japan. And we also explained how we look at religions related to these events.

That's all for today. We hope you enjoyed our program. Thank you for watching.

MISSION 06

LEARN WORDS, PHRASES & EXPRESSIONS

プロジェクトに使えそうな語句や表現を学び、原稿作成に活用しましょう。

WORDS & PHRASES

1 行事・祝祭日

annual event / St. Valentine's Day / White Day / the Dolls Festival / *hanami* (cherry blossom viewing) / the Star Festival / the Bon Festival / New Year's Eve / national holiday / New Year's Day / Coming-of-Age Day / Children's Day / Respect-for-the-Aged Day / Culture Day / Labor Thanksgiving Day / the Golden Week holiday

2 文化・芸能

tea ceremony / flower arrangement / *kabuki* / *noh* / *rakugo* (comic story-telling) / *sumo* / *haiku* / *ukiyo-e* / *bonsai* / *anime* / *manga* / *cosplay* / J-pop

3 その他

omotenashi (hospitality) / *Bushido* / Shintoism / Buddhism / *sasshi* (tacit communication) / *wa* (harmony) / *wabi* and *sabi* / *mottainai* / *honne* and *tatemae*

EXPRESSIONS

1「日本独特の『もの』の説明」

an offering box <u>called</u> *saisen-bako* / *omikuji*, a fortune-telling paper / *Otoshidama* is gift money <u>in English</u>.

2「複雑な概念の説明」

... is like ... / For example, ... / Just as people in western countries ..., ... / It literally means ...

PRESENTATION TECHNIQUES

" 日本独自の「もの」をor ... で説明 "

SAMPLE の第 7 ブロック *osechi-ryori*, **or** traditional New Year's dishes **SAMPLE の第 14 ブロック** *otoshidama*, **or** gift money given to children by their parents **SAMPLE の第 15 ブロック** *hatsumode*, **or** the first visit to a shrine	▶ 「おせち料理」、「お年玉」、「初詣」のように英語圏に存在しない「もの」に言及する場合は、日本語の後に or でつなぎ、英語訳を加えて説明ができます。この or は「すなわち」、「言い換えると」のような意味です。

DECIDE WHAT YOU TALK ABOUT

サンプル・プレゼンテーションを参考に、以下の要領で内容を決めましょう。

1. リーダー（グループのまとめ役）とMC（司会進行役）を決める。
2. MCは進行役に加え、自分のPOINTも担当する。
3. グループで協議し、自然な論旨が展開できるよう各自のPOINTを決める。
4. 決まった内容を下の表に記入し、グループで共有する。

【サンプル・プレゼンテーション】

	内　容	担当	時間
INTRODUCTION	Greeting / Overview	MC	0'15"
POINT 1	Christmas	恵美	1'00"
	transition	MC	0'10"
POINT 2	Year-end	猛	1'00"
	transition	MC	0'10"
POINT 3	New Year's holiday	良二	1'00"
	transition	MC	0'10"
POINT 4	Our Unique Ideas about Religion	華蓮	1'00"
CONCLUSION	Wrap-Up / Greeting	MC	0'15"

【あなたのグループのプレゼンテーション】

	内　容	担当	時間
INTRODUCTION	Greeting / Overview	MC	0'15"
POINT 1			1'00"
	transition	MC	0'10"
POINT 2			1'00"
	transition	MC	0'10"
POINT 3			1'00"
	transition	MC	0'10"
POINT 4			1'00"
CONCLUSION	Wrap-Up / Greeting	MC	0'15"

PREPARE YOUR SPEECH MESSAGE

【あなたのグループのプレゼンテーション】を元に、原稿を作成しましょう（パソコンのWordに直接書き込んでも可）。

MISSION 06

1 主要な英文を作成しましょう。

▼「日本独特の文化や習慣」について：
We'll explain our interesting event of... / We'll talk about our unique culture of...などを使って

```
```

▼「日本独特のもの」について：（日本語のローマ字書き）or（英語での説明）
It is called ... in English. などを使って

```
```

▼「複雑な概念」について：
It is like ... / It literally means ...などを使って

```
```

2 作成した主要な英文を中心に枝葉をつけて、自分の担当箇所の原稿（150語前後）を完成させましょう。

3 原稿の点検

作成した原稿（Speech Message）を下のリストで点検しましょう。

SPEECH MESSAGEの点検	点検のポイント	チェック
① Number of Words	時間に対して語数は適量か	☐
② Plain English	平易な英語で書かれているか	☐
③ Rhetorical Questions	聴衆への問い掛けはあるか	☐
④ Logical	論理的に書かれているか	☐
⑤ Interesting (Funny)	興味深い内容になっているか	☐

4 MC担当者は進行のための原稿も準備しましょう。

◎【あなたのグループのプレゼンテーション】を元に、
　グループ全体のINTRODUCTIONとCONCLUSIONの原稿を準備する。

◎【あなたのグループのプレゼンテーション】を元に、プレゼンターとプレゼンターの橋渡し
　（transition）の原稿も準備する（P.32のPRESENTATION TECHNIQUESを参照）。

HOMEWORK

① 原稿が未完成の場合は完成させ、点検する。
② 次回のスライド作成のための材料（写真、イラストなど）を準備する。

WEEK 2　PREPARATION 2

WEEK2の準備をします。スライドを作成し、リハーサルを行います。

PREPARE YOUR VISUAL MESSAGE

1 スライドの構成と内容 ➡ （P.35を参照）

2 スライドの作成 ➡ （P.35を参照）

3 今回のプロジェクトでの工夫：写真の中に文字を書き込む

写真の中に文字を書き入れて、より効果的なスライドを作りましょう。
ツールバーから［挿入］➡［テキストボックス］➡ カーソルをドラッグしてテキストボックスを作る ➡ キーワードを書き込む ➡ テキストボックス上で右クリック ➡［塗りつぶし］から見やすい背景色を選ぶ。

People throw money into *saisen-bako*, or an offering box,（中略）Some people also buy *omikuji*, a fortune- telling paper,（後略）

背景を白にした例

4 スライドの点検

VISUAL MESSAGE の点検	点検のポイント	チェック
① Number of Slides	スライドの枚数は適当か	☐
② Key Words/Numbers	重要な語句や数字は書かれているか	☐
③ Images (Photos, Illustrations)	写真やイラストは効果的に使えているか	☐
④ Charts/Graphs	図表やグラフは効果的に使えているか	☐

5 ひとつのファイルにまとめる ➡ （P.36を参照）

REHEARSE

以下の要領でグループでのリハーサルを行いましょう。

1 原稿を覚える

グループ単位でPCにスライドを写しながら、原稿を覚える。1回目、2回目と回数を重ねるごとに原稿から目を離し、スライドだけをヒントに英語が口をついて出てくるまで練習を繰り返す。

2 相互チェック ➡ （P.36を参照）

点検項目	評価					コメント
❶ SPEECH MESSAGE	1	2	3	4	5	
Plain English	1	2	3	4	5	
Rhetorical Questions	1	2	3	4	5	
Logical	1	2	3	4	5	
Interesting (Funny)	1	2	3	4	5	
❷ VISUAL MESSAGE (Slides)	1	2	3	4	5	
Key Words/Numbers	1	2	3	4	5	
Images (Photos, Illustrations)	1	2	3	4	5	
Charts/Graphs	1	2	3	4	5	
❸ PHYSICAL MESSAGE	1	2	3	4	5	
Voice Inflection	1	2	3	4	5	
Eye Contact	1	2	3	4	5	
Hands (Pointer)	1	2	3	4	5	
Posture	1	2	3	4	5	

❸ グループの時間管理（Time Management）

所定の時間内にグループ内のメンバーが全員発表できるように、時間管理をしましょう。
 ➡（P.37を参照）

❹ 立ち位置 ➡ （P.38を参照）

HOMEWORK

① リハーサルの結果、修正の必要があれば修正する。
② 各自が原稿を見ずにスラスラ言えるようになるまで練習する。
③ グループで発表用の配布資料を準備する（P.24参照）。

WEEK 3 PRESENTATION

プロジェクトの発表を行います。発表の後に自己評価をしましょう。

GIVE A PRESENTATION

- ☐ 配布資料を配る。
- ☐ 原稿を見ずに発表を行う。
- ☐ 制限時間(5分)内にグループ全体を収める。
- ☐ 発表前にスマホ等によるビデオ撮影をクラスメートに依頼する。

EVALUATE YOUR OWN PRESENTATION

撮った映像を見て自己評価をし、次のステップアップにつなげましょう。

評価項目	評 価					コメント
❶ SPEECH MESSAGE	1	2	3	4	5	
Plain English	1	2	3	4	5	
Rhetorical Questions	1	2	3	4	5	
Logical	1	2	3	4	5	
Interesting (Funny)	1	2	3	4	5	
❷ VISUAL MESSAGE (Slides)	1	2	3	4	5	
Key Words/Numbers	1	2	3	4	5	
Images (Photos, Illustrations)	1	2	3	4	5	
Charts/Graphs	1	2	3	4	5	
❸ PHYSICAL MESSAGE	1	2	3	4	5	
Voice Inflection	1	2	3	4	5	
Eye Contact	1	2	3	4	5	
Hands (Pointer)	1	2	3	4	5	
Posture	1	2	3	4	5	

特記事項

HOMEWORK

① MISSION 7のサンプル・プレゼンテーションを読む。
② LEARN WORDS, PHRASES & EXPRESSIONS (P.94)に目を通す。
③ 個人的な悩みや社会の問題などについて2、3考えてくる。

MISSION 07
SOLVE PROBLEMS

MISSION 07 では…

問題解決のためのグループ・プロジェクトです。
多くの人に共通する個人的な悩みや問題、あるいは、社会の問題を取り上げ、
その解決策をグループで議論し、提案します。

CAN-DO LIST

ENGLISH SKILLS

- 個人の問題や社会問題を英語で「議論」できる。
- 英語で論理的な展開を行うことができる。
- 問題解決のための「提案」(We suggest … など) ができる。

PRESENTATION SKILLS

- 「議論」のプレゼンテーションができる。
- 説明的なスライドを作成することができる。
- グループで論理的な展開ができる。

WEEK 1　PREPARATION 1

プロジェクトの内容と準備の要領を確認し、**WEEK1** の準備を行います。

" MISSION 07 "
SOLVE PROBLEMS

設　定 ▶ 留学生が在籍するクラス
目　的 ▶ 個人の悩みや社会の問題を取り上げ、解決策を提案する。
形　態 ▶ グループ（4人）
時　間 ▶ 5分（グループで）
準　備 ▶ **WEEK 1** … サンプルを読む、語彙・表現を学ぶ、グループで打ち合わせる、原稿を書く。
　　　　WEEK 2 … スライドを作成し、グループで1つにまとめる、リハーサルを行う。
　　　　WEEK 3 … グループで発表する。

LEARN FROM THE SAMPLE　 Audio 11

SAMPLE

▶ **MC(Miyu):** Hello, everyone. We're Group 3.

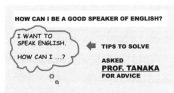

▶ You often hear people say, "I want to speak English, but I can't. How can I be a good speaker?" Probably, many of you have the same problem. In our presentation, we're going to give you some tips to solve this problem. For this project, we asked Prof. Tanaka for some advice.

MISSION 07

► First, we'll talk about vocabulary and grammar. Then, we'll show you some effective ways to practice speaking. And finally, we'll also tell you how you can improve your listening. Will you begin, Kazuya?

OVERVIEW
1. VOCABULARY
2. GRAMMAR
3. HOW TO PRACTICE SPEAKING
4. HOW TO IMPROVE LISTENING

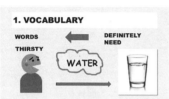

► **Kazuya:** OK. In order to speak, you definitely need to know words. When you're thirsty and want something to drink, you say "Water!" right? Even if you're excellent in grammar, you can't get water if you don't know the word.

► Then, how many words do you need? According to Prof. Tanaka, you should learn 2,000 basic words as a first step. It's not really a big vocabulary. You memorized 4,000, 5,000 or even more for university entrance exams.

1. VOCABULARY

THE POINT IS ... KEEP 2,000 WORDS ACTIVE & READY

GET THE **RIGHT WORD THE MOMENT** YOU NEED IT

► The point is you have to be able to get the right word the moment you need it. Unlike reading or writing, you have no time to look for it in a dictionary. You have to get it in a moment. To make it possible, you need to keep the 2,000 words always active and ready. Don't let them sleep. That's the point about vocabulary.

MC(Miyu): 2,000 active words ... OK. How about grammar, Akane?

► **Akane:** As Kazuya said, if you want water, just say "Water!" and you'll get it. But our communication is not always that simple. You say "Water," and some people may ask, "Water? What do you mean?"

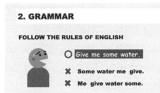

▶ Then, you'll have to add some words and say, "Give me some water," for example. This time, everyone will understand you. This has to be "Give me some water," not "Some water me give" or "Me give water some." You have to follow the rules for word order of English. You have to follow many other rules, too — that is, grammar.

▶ Prof. Tanaka suggests you understand and remember 20 basic rules. They are mostly the rules you learned in junior high school. If you don't remember them well, just review the textbooks you used.

MC(Miyu): Thank you, Akane.
Now, the main point: how you practice speaking. I'll tell you two ways of doing it.

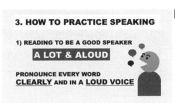

▶ **Miyu:** One of them is reading —— reading to be a good speaker. You have to read a lot and aloud. Don't read silently, but pronounce every single word clearly in a loud voice.

▶ Read many books this way. "Many English books? No way. I've never finished an English book. How can I do it?" you may ask. Here's the answer: choose easy books called Graded Readers. They are English books but are rewritten in easy English. You'll find them in the school library and bookstores.

▶ The other way we recommend is "One-minute Speaking to Yourself." You speak to yourself in English for one minute.

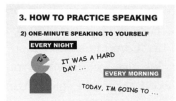

▶ Make it a daily habit. For example, you do it every night in bed before you sleep, looking back over the day, or every morning on your way to school, thinking about your plans for the day. In a month or two, you'll find yourself much better at speaking English.

MC(Miyu): OK, so far? There's one more thing you need. It's listening skill. Takuma will tell you about it.

▶ **Takuma:** All right. To be a good speaker of English, you need to be a good listener. You need to be able to understand what the other person says. It takes a lot of practice, but the thing you have to do is very simple: just listen — listen a lot.

▶ We recommend you use the Internet. You'll find tons of materials that you can use for the practice. There're Web TV news shows, YouTube videos, free online lectures, and more. You can watch them repeatedly.

▶ If they come with scripts or captions, read them after watching. They'll help you understand. Also, with the scripts or captions, you can see where you didn't understand and what words you couldn't catch.

▶ I think everybody has a smartphone. It means you can practice on the train, in a coffee shop, or even in the bathroom.

WRAP-UP
1. VOCABULARY
   2,000 basic words
2. GRAMMAR
   20 basic rules
3. HOW TO PRACTICE SPEAKING
   Reading many easy books aloud
   "One-minute Speaking to Yourself"
4. HOW TO IMPROVE LISTENING
   Use the Internet

▶ **MC(Miyu):** Great idea, Takuma.

Now, you've got everything. Let's review. To be a good speaker of English, you need to know 2,000 basic words and 20 basic rules of grammar. And for speaking practice, we introduced two approaches: reading many easy books aloud and "One-minute Speaking to Yourself" practice. And for listening practice, we recommended the use of the Internet.

We hope all these tips will be a good solution. Thank you.

LEARN WORDS, PHRASES & EXPRESSIONS

プロジェクトに使えそうな語句や表現を学び、原稿作成に活用しましょう。

WORDS & PHRASES

1 学生の問題

have no friends / do not have a girlfriend / do not have a boyfriend / too busy working part-time / can't find a good part-time job / have little time to study / too much homework / boring classes / can't raise my TOEIC® score / have nothing interesting / stressful job hunting / have no idea of what to do after university / expensive school fees / can't stop smoking / suicide

2 社会問題

aging society / declining birth rate / declining marriage rate / job opportunities for women / working environment for women / work-life balance / "black" businesses / increasing gap between the rich and the poor / energy issues / nuclear power plants / drug abuse / addicted to smartphones / trouble on SNS / crowded trains / expensive housing / the Constitution of Japan

EXPRESSIONS

1 「問題の現状を伝える」

We hear many students say … / You often read in newspapers that … / Many people have a problem with … / have a problem that … / … is becoming a social issue. / Experts say …

2 「重要なポイント」

The (important) point is … / …. That's the point. / What matters is …

3 「問題解決の提案」

We suggest … / We recommend … / One of the ways to solve the problem is … / A possible solution is … / Why don't you …? / You should …

PRESENTATION TECHNIQUES
" 論理的な展開をはっきり示す "

SAMPLE の第4〜6ブロック **In order to** speak, you definitely need to know words. … **Then**, how many words do you need? … **The point is** … **To make it possible**, you need to …	聴衆に「議論」を分かりやすく伝えるためには、話を論理的に展開する必要があります。サンプルにあるように、言葉ではっきりと議論の展開を示しましょう。

DECIDE WHAT YOU TALK ABOUT

サンプル・プレゼンテーションを参考に、以下の要領で内容を決めましょう。

1. リーダー（グループのまとめ役）とMC（司会進行役）を決める。
2. MCは進行役に加え、自分のPOINTも担当する。
3. グループで協議し、自然な論旨が展開できるよう各自のPOINTを決める。
4. 決まった内容を下の表に記入し、グループで共有する。

【サンプル・プレゼンテーション】

	内　容	担当	時間
INTRODUCTION	Greeting / Overview	MC	0'15"
POINT 1	Vocabulary	和也	1'00"
	transition	MC	0'10"
POINT 2	Grammar	茜	1'00"
	transition	MC	0'10"
POINT 3	How to Practice Speaking	美優	1'00"
	transition	MC	0'10"
POINT 4	How to Improve Listening	琢磨	1'00"
CONCLUSION	Wrap-Up / Greeting	MC	0'15"

【あなたのグループのプレゼンテーション】

	内　容	担当	時間
INTRODUCTION	Greeting / Overview	MC	0'15"
POINT 1			1'00"
	transition	MC	0'10"
POINT 2			1'00"
	transition	MC	0'10"
POINT 3			1'00"
	transition	MC	0'10"
POINT 4			1'00"
CONCLUSION	Wrap-Up / Greeting	MC	0'15"

PREPARE YOUR SPEECH MESSAGE

【あなたのグループのプレゼンテーション】を元に、原稿を作成しましょう（パソコンのWordに直接書き込んでも可）。

MISSION 07

1 主要な英文を作成しましょう。

▼「問題の現状」について：
　We hear many students say ... / ... is becoming a social issue. などを使って

```
```

▼「重要なポイント」について：
　The point is ... / The important thing is ... などを使って

```
```

▼「問題解決の提案」について：
　We suggest ... / You should ... などを使って

```
```

2 作成した主要な英文を中心に枝葉をつけて、自分の担当箇所の原稿（150語前後）を完成させましょう。

3 原稿の点検

作成した原稿（Speech Message）を「点検リスト」で点検しましょう。

SPEECH MESSAGEの点検	点検のポイント	チェック
① Number of Words	時間に対して語数は適量か	☐
② Plain English	平易な英語で書かれているか	☐
③ Rhetorical Questions	聴衆への問い掛けはあるか	☐
④ Logical	論理的に書かれているか	☐
⑤ Interesting (Funny)	興味深い内容になっているか	☐

4 MC担当者は進行のための原稿も準備しましょう。

◎【あなたのグループのプレゼンテーション】を元に、
　グループ全体のINTRODUCTIONとCONCLUSIONの原稿を準備する。

◎【あなたのグループのプレゼンテーション】を元に、プレゼンターとプレゼンターの橋渡し
　（transition）の原稿も準備する（P.32のPRESENTATION TECHNIQUESを参照）。

HOMEWORK

① 原稿が未完成の場合は完成させ、点検する。
② 次回のスライド作成のための材料（写真、イラストなど）を準備する。

WEEK 2　PREPARATION 2

WEEK2 の準備をします。スライドを作成し、リハーサルを行います。

PREPARE YOUR VISUAL MESSAGE

1 スライドの構成と内容 ➡ （P.35を参照）

2 スライドの作成 ➡ （P.35を参照）

3 今回のプロジェクトでの工夫：「描画」でアナログ的なイメージを
ときどき「描画」でアナログ的なイメージを演出してみましょう。
ツールバーから［描画］をクリックし、ペン、色、太さを選びます。手書きの感覚で描けます。

… People say, "I want to speak English, but I can't How can I …?"

例：「吹き出し」を描く

4 スライドの点検

VISUAL MESSAGE の点検	点検のポイント	チェック
① Number of Slides	スライドの枚数は適当か	☐
② Key Words/Numbers	重要な語句や数字は書かれているか	☐
③ Images (Photos, Illustrations)	写真やイラストは効果的に使えているか	☐
④ Charts / Graphs	図表やグラフは効果的に使えているか	☐

5 ひとつのファイルにまとめる ➡ （P.36を参照）

REHEARSE

以下の要領でグループでのリハーサルを行いましょう。

1 原稿を覚える
グループ単位でPCにスライドを写しながら、原稿を覚える。1回目、2回目と回数を重ねるごとに原稿から目を離し、スライドだけをヒントに英語が口をついて出てくるまで練習を繰り返す。

2 相互チェック ➡ （P.36を参照）

MISSION 07

点検項目	評価					コメント
❶ SPEECH MESSAGE	1	2	3	4	5	
Plain English	1	2	3	4	5	
Rhetorical Questions	1	2	3	4	5	
Logical	1	2	3	4	5	
Interesting (Funny)	1	2	3	4	5	
❷ VISUAL MESSAGE (Slides)	1	2	3	4	5	
Key Words/Numbers	1	2	3	4	5	
Images (Photos, Illustrations)	1	2	3	4	5	
Charts/Graphs	1	2	3	4	5	
❸ PHYSICAL MESSAGE	1	2	3	4	5	
Voice Inflection	1	2	3	4	5	
Eye Contact	1	2	3	4	5	
Hands (Pointer)	1	2	3	4	5	
Posture	1	2	3	4	5	

❸ **グループの時間管理（Time Management）**
所定の時間内にグループ内のメンバーが全員発表できるように、時間管理をしましょう。
➡ （P.37を参照）

❹ **立ち位置** ➡ （P.38を参照）

HOMEWORK

① リハーサルの結果、修正の必要があれば修正する。
② 各自が原稿を見ずにスラスラ言えるようになるまで練習する。
③ グループで発表用の配布資料を準備する（P.24参照）。

WEEK 3　PRESENTATION

プロジェクトの発表を行います。発表の後に自己評価をしましょう。

GIVE A PRESENTATION

☐ 配布資料を配る。
☐ 原稿を見ずに発表を行う。
☐ 制限時間(5分)内にグループ全体を収める。
☐ 発表前にスマホ等によるビデオ撮影をクラスメートに依頼する。

EVALUATE YOUR OWN PRESENTATION

撮った映像を見て自己評価をし、次のステップアップにつなげましょう。

評価項目	評価					コメント
❶ SPEECH MESSAGE	1	2	3	4	5	
Plain English	1	2	3	4	5	
Rhetorical Questions	1	2	3	4	5	
Logical	1	2	3	4	5	
Interesting (Funny)	1	2	3	4	5	
❷ VISUAL MESSAGE (Slides)	1	2	3	4	5	
Key Words/Numbers	1	2	3	4	5	
Images (Photos, Illustrations)	1	2	3	4	5	
Charts/Graphs	1	2	3	4	5	
❸ PHYSICAL MESSAGE	1	2	3	4	5	
Voice Inflection	1	2	3	4	5	
Eye Contact	1	2	3	4	5	
Hands (Pointer)	1	2	3	4	5	
Posture	1	2	3	4	5	

特記事項

HOMEWORK

① MISSION 8のサンプル・プレゼンテーションを読む。
② LEARN WORDS, PHRASES & EXPRESSIONS (P.105)に目を通す。
③ 自分の将来の計画(夢、職業など)について考えてくる。

MISSION 08
TALK ABOUT YOUR FUTURE PLANS

MISSION 08 では…

あなたの将来の計画や夢について語ります。大学生活も含めて将来計画していることや、心に抱いている夢などをできるだけ具体的に話しましょう。

具体的なビジョンを持っていない人は、これを機に考えてみましょう。

CAN-DO LIST

ENGLISH SKILLS

- 将来の計画や夢について英語で原稿を準備し、発表することができる。
- 「希望・願望」の表現（My dream is to be …）が適切にできる。
- 就職、職業関係の語彙・表現（apply for a job at …など）を必要に応じて使うことができる。

PRESENTATION SKILLS

- 自分の将来についての「情報伝達」ができる。
- 時系列で説明的なスライドを作成することができる。
- 将来の計画や夢を楽しく表現できる。

WEEK 1　PREPARATION 1

プロジェクトの内容と準備の要領を確認し、**WEEK1** の準備を行います。

> **" MISSION 08 "**
> **TALK ABOUT YOUR FUTURE PLANS**
>
> 設 定 ▶ 留学生が在籍するクラス
> 目 的 ▶ 自分の将来の計画や夢について、実現するために
> 　　　　① 今できること ② その先の具体的な計画などを述べる。
> 形 態 ▶ 個人
> 時 間 ▶ 1分（2分＊）　＊余裕のあるクラスは発表を2分間にし、3週間で準備し、WEEK4で「発表」としてもよい。
> 準 備 ▶ **WEEK 1** … サンプルを読む。
> 　　　　**WEEK 2** … スライドを作成し、リハーサルを行う。
> 　　　　**WEEK 3** … 発表する。

LEARN FROM THE SAMPLES

SAMPLE 1　🔊 Audio 12

▶ Hello, I'm Hideki Miwa. I'll talk about my future plans.

▶ I'm a first-year student, majoring in computer science. After I graduate, I'd like to work as a computer engineer.

MISSION 08

▶ I have always been interested in computers since I first played a computer game when I was eight. Since then, I have learned a lot about computers.

▶ I think I know more about computers than most people, but it's not enough to work as a professional. So, in addition to the regular classes, I'm thinking of joining an internship program at an IT company next year.

▶ When I finally graduate, I want to get a job at an IT company. My ultimate goal, however, is to start up my own business.

▶ And someday, I'd like to make something that will surprise the world, like Bill Gates and Steve Jobs did.

▶ Do you think I'm a dreamer? Well, *they* realized their dreams. Why can't *I*?

TALK ABOUT YOUR FUTURE PLANS

SAMPLE 2 Audio 13

▶ Hello. I'm Yuka Takahashi. Let me tell you about my future plans or dreams.

▶ One of the dreams that I've had since I was a little girl is to be a beautiful, lovely bride like a princess.

▶ To make it come true, I'm studying hard at university. I have to be a nice, well-educated, mature woman so my prince will come to find me.

▶ Another dream is a job I want to do after I graduate. It's directly related to my first dream — a wedding planner.

▶ I want to work at a hotel in its wedding section, where I help young couples plan their happiest event.

▶ If I close my eyes, I can see a beautifully decorated ballroom where a bride and a groom are smiling happily with their families, friends, and many other guests.

▶ And I'm in a corner of the ballroom, making sure everything is going well. They're my future dreams. Thank you.

LEARN WORDS, PHRASES & EXPRESSIONS

プロジェクトに使えそうな語句や表現を学び、原稿作成に活用しましょう。

WORDS & PHRASES

1 職業
office worker / accountant / counselor / engineer / flight attendant /
bank clerk / management consultant / lawyer / travel agent /
computer programmer / wedding planner / CPA / tax accountant /
high school teacher / freelance writer

2 業種
IT industry / advertisement industry / travel industry / financial world /
automobile manufacturer / entertainment market / high-tech company /
mass media / publishing industry

3 時期
after university / before 30 / in my early 30s / around 40 / after retirement

4 その他
get married / have a family / live in a foreign country /
make my dream come true / realize my dream / ultimate goal

EXPRESSIONS

1 「希望・願望」
In the future, I want to … / I'd like to … / My dream is to … /
One of the dreams that I have is to … / I'm hoping to … / If possible, …

2 「取り組み」
I'm studying … hard / I'm thinking of ～ ing … / In order to realize it, I need to …

3 「就職・その他」
apply for a job at… / send a resume to… / have a job interview /
take an employment exam of ABC company / get a job at … / work as …

PRESENTATION TECHNIQUES
" 声に抑揚をつける "

SAMPLE 1 の第6ブロック
Do you think I'm a dreamer? Well, **they** realized their dreams. Why can't **I**?

SAMPLE 2 の第2ブロック
One of the dreams … is to be a **beautiful**, **lovely** bride like a princess.

▶ 私たちは英語を平坦に話しがちです。語句の重要度に応じて声の強弱、高低、長短を調整しましょう。例えば左の斜字体の部分や下線部などは、強く、高く、長めに発音してその語句を強調します。

DECIDE WHAT YOU TALK ABOUT

サンプル・プレゼンテーションを参考にブレーンストーミングを行い、あなた自身のプレゼンテーションの内容を決めましょう（下の【あなたのプレゼンテーション】にメモ）。

【SAMPLE1のプレゼンテーション】

タイトル	将来の計画： コンピューターエンジニア
INTRODUCTION	挨　拶
Point 1 自己紹介 卒 業 後	１年 コンピューター専攻 コンピューターエンジニア
Point 2 取り組み	８歳からファミコン 以来独学
Point 3 仕　事	卒業後：IT企業 最終ゴール：自分の会社
CONCLUSION	ビル・ゲイツ、 スティーブ・ジョブズの ように

【あなたのプレゼンテーション】

PREPARE YOUR SPEECH MESSAGE

【あなたのプレゼンテーション】を元に、原稿を作成しましょう（パソコンのWordに直接書き込んでも可）。

1 主要な英文を作成しましょう。

▼「希望・願望」について：
　I'd like to ... / My dream is to ...などを使って

▼「具体的な取り組み」について：
　I'm ~ing ... / I'm thinking of ~ing ... / I need to ...などを使って

▼「仕事・夢」について：
　I'd like to work at ... / I want to be ...などを使って

2 作成した主要な英文を中心に枝葉をつけて、INTRODUCTION, BODY, CONCLUSIONの構成を整えて、原稿全体（150語前後）を完成させましょう。

3 原稿の点検
　作成した原稿（Speech Message）を「点検リスト」でチェックしましょう。

SPEECH MESSAGEの点検	点検のポイント	チェック
① Number of Words	時間に対して語数は適量か	☐
② Plain English	平易な英語で書かれているか	☐
③ Rhetorical Questions	聴衆への問い掛けはあるか	☐
④ Logical	論理的に書かれているか	☐
⑤ Interesting (Funny)	興味深い内容になっているか	☐

HOMEWORK

① 原稿が未完成の場合は完成させ、点検する。
② 次回のスライド作成のための材料（写真、イラストなど）を準備する。

WEEK 2　PREPARATION 2

WEEK 2の準備をします。スライドを作成し、リハーサルを行います。

PREPARE YOUR VISUAL MESSAGE

■ スライドの作成

サンプル・プレゼンテーションのスライドを参考に、あなた自身のスライドを原稿と照らし合わせながら作成しましょう。

【SAMPLE1のスライドの構成と内容】

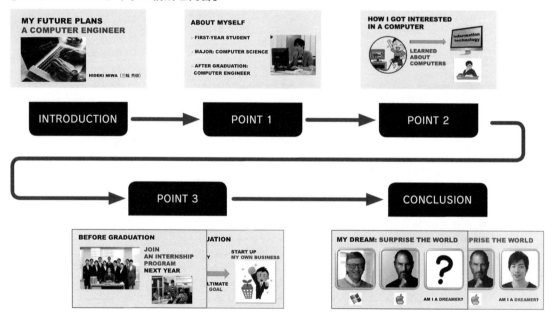

2 今回のプロジェクトでの工夫：アニメーションを使う。

アニメーションを使ってインパクトの強いスライドを作りましょう。
ツールバーから[アニメーション]➡[アニメーションの追加]➡必要なアニメーションを選択する。

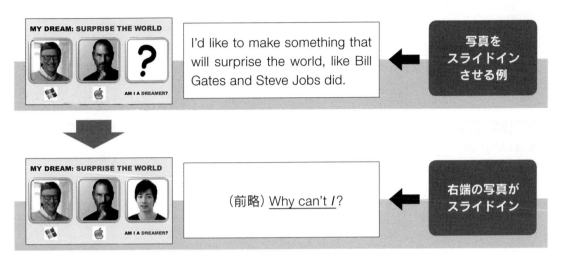

3 スライドの点検

作成したスライド（Visual Message）を「点検リスト」でチェックしましょう。

VISUAL MESSAGE の点検	点検のポイント	チェック
① Number of Slides	スライドの枚数は適当か	☐
② Key Words/Numbers	重要な語句や数字は書かれているか	☐
③ Images (Photos, Illustrations)	写真やイラストは効果的に使えているか	☐
④ Charts/Graphs	図表やグラフは効果的に使えているか	☐

REHEARSE

以下の要領でリハーサルをしましょう。

1 原稿を覚える

自分のPCでスライドを見ながら（ツールバーで[スライドショー]）原稿を覚える。1回目、2回目と回数を重ねるごとに原稿から目を離し、スライドだけをヒントに英語が口をついて出てくるまで練習を繰り返す。

2 ペア練習 （A：プレゼンター、B：聞き手）

ペアを組んで各自3回リハーサルを行う。プレゼンターは自分のPCでスライドを見せながら発表し、聞き手は「点検リスト」でプレゼンターのパフォーマンスをチェックする（スマホ等でビデオ撮影をしてもよい）。

MISSION 08

	A	B
1回目	発　表	Aが話す英語（Speech Message）に焦点をあててコメントする。
2回目	発　表	スライド（Visual Message）に焦点をあててコメントする。
3回目	発　表	声、目、手、姿勢（Physical Message）に焦点をあててコメントする。

引き続きAとBは役割を換え、同様の練習を行う。

点 検 項 目	評　価					コ　メ　ン　ト
❶ SPEECH MESSAGE	1	2	3	4	5	
Plain English	1	2	3	4	5	
Rhetorical Questions	1	2	3	4	5	
Logical	1	2	3	4	5	
Interesting (Funny)	1	2	3	4	5	
❷ VISUAL MESSAGE (Slides)	1	2	3	4	5	
Key Words/Numbers	1	2	3	4	5	
Images (Photos, Illustrations)	1	2	3	4	5	
Charts/Graphs	1	2	3	4	5	
❸ PHYSICAL MESSAGE	1	2	3	4	5	
Voice Inflection	1	2	3	4	5	
Eye Contact	1	2	3	4	5	
Hands (Pointer)	1	2	3	4	5	
Posture	1	2	3	4	5	

HOMEWORK

① リハーサルの結果、修正の必要があれば修正する。
② 原稿を見ずにスラスラ言えるようになるまで練習する。
③ 発表用の配布資料を準備する（P.24参照）。

WEEK 3 PRESENTATION

プロジェクトの発表を行います。発表の後に自己評価をしましょう。

GIVE A PRESENTATION

- ☐ 配付資料を配る。
- ☐ 原稿を見ずに発表を行う。
- ☐ 制限時間（1分）内に全体を収める。
- ☐ 発表前にスマホ等によるビデオ撮影をクラスメートに依頼する。

EVALUATE YOUR OWN PRESENTATION

撮った映像を見て自己評価をし、次のステップアップにつなげましょう。

評価項目	評価					コメント
❶ SPEECH MESSAGE	1	2	3	4	5	
Plain English	1	2	3	4	5	
Rhetorical Questions	1	2	3	4	5	
Logical	1	2	3	4	5	
Interesting (Funny)	1	2	3	4	5	
❷ VISUAL MESSAGE (Slides)	1	2	3	4	5	
Key Words/Numbers	1	2	3	4	5	
Images (Photos, Illustrations)	1	2	3	4	5	
Charts/Graphs	1	2	3	4	5	
❸ PHYSICAL MESSAGE	1	2	3	4	5	
Voice Inflection	1	2	3	4	5	
Eye Contact	1	2	3	4	5	
Hands (Pointer)	1	2	3	4	5	
Posture	1	2	3	4	5	

特記事項

HOMEWORK

今回で最終回になりますのでHOMEWORKはありません。
今まで学習したことを将来に生かせるよう、もう一度しっかりと復習しましょう。

▼写真・装画
《表紙》
© プラナ/PIXTA

《本文》
Introduction © Noboru Matsuoka
Mission 1 © ABC/PIXTA ; © blackie0335/PIXTA ; © Caito/PIXTA ; © Fast&Slow/PIXTA ; © grycikua/PIXTA ; © hiro/PIXTA ; © IYO/PIXTA ; © kazu.ne.jp/PIXTA ; © kotoru/PIXTA ; © msv/PIXTA ; © SENBA/PIXTA ; © xiangtao/PIXTA ; © zakiyamac/PIXTA ; © ツネオ MP/PIXTA ; © 山梨市
Mission 2 © amaguma/PIXTA ; © freeangle/PIXTA ; © Hiroki Saito（玄龍ラーメン）; © narak0rn/PIXTA ; © Noboru Matsuoka ; © perori/PIXTA ; © shiga masato/PIXTA ; ©【Tig.】Tokyo image groups/PIXTA ; © yanmo/PIXTA ; © wavebreakmedia/PIXTA ; © まちゃー /PIXTA
Mission 3 © ABC/PIXTA ; © AIR/PIXTA ; © blackie0335/PIXTA ; © chepilev/PIXTA ; © Graphs/PIXTA ; © jet/PIXTA ; © J6HQL/PIXTA ; © KAORU/PIXTA ; © kuro3/PIXTA ; © mag/PIXTA ; © Nutria/PIXTA ; © 阿野陽 /PIXTA © うえむらのぶこ ; © 極楽蜻蛉 /PIXTA ; © ごりっぱ /PIXTA © ジャバ /PIXTA ; © チビタム /PIXTA ; © とんとん /PIXTA ; © パームツリー /PIXTA ; © 風景 /PIXTA ; © 悠太郎 /PIXTA ; © Curioso/Shutterstock, Inc. ; © Kekyalyaynen/Shutterstock, Inc. ; © KP Photograph / Shutterstock, Inc. ; © Parote Patrungsee/Shutterstock, Inc. ; © Vincent St. Thomas/Shutterstock, Inc.
Mission 4 © hagamera/PIXTA ; © Hisao/PIXTA ; © kahon/PIXTA ; © kiki/PIXTA ; © mii/PIXTA ; © shanaou_pro/PIXTA ; © shico2000/PIXTA ; © Stickami/PIXTA ; © YsPhoto/PIXTA ; © H・東洋 /PIXTA ; © かげぼうし /PIXTA ; © ケンケン /PIXTA ; © さにべい /PIXTA ; © ばりろく /PIXTA ; © まっき /PIXTA ; © Oscity/Shutterstock, Inc. ; © Lucky-photographer/Shutterstock, Inc.
Mission 5 © japan007/PIXTA ; © Mengpong Akane/PIXTA ; © Noboru Matsuoka ; © tsuppy/PIXTA ; © ちいこ /PIXTA ; © 大阪・春風会合気道 小川恵理子 弐段
Mission 6 © Dot Color/PIXTA ; © ema/PIXTA ; © Garnett/PIXTA ; © genki/PIXTA ; © HALI/PIXTA ; © HAMA/PIXTA ; © Hungry Works/PIXTA ; © kazu/PIXTA ; © Kimi/PIXTA ; © msv/PIXTA; © NISH/PIXTA ; © NOBU/PIXTA ; © robbie/PIXTA ; © saki/PIXTA ; © shin28/PIXTA ; © StudioR310/PIXTA ; © Violet/PIXTA ; © YNS/PIXTA ; © YUMIK/PIXTA ; © H・東洋 /PIXTA ; © オクケン /PIXTA ; © くま社長 /PIXTA ; © スムース /PIXTA ; © そば /PIXTA ; © マーボー /PIXTA ; © まちゃー /PIXTA ; © 夢華 /PIXTA ; © r.nagy/Shutterstock, Inc.
Mission 7 © mylisa/PIXTA ; © Noboru Matsuoka
Mission 8 © Fast&Slow/PIXTA ; © HHImages/PIXTA ; © kou/PIXTA ; © Ushico/PIXTA ; © xiangtao/PIXTA ; © ケイアール /PIXTA ; © す〜ロン /PIXTA ; © スコッティ /PIXTA ; © プラナ /PIXTA

JPCA 本書は日本出版著作権協会（JPCA）が委託管理する著作物です。
複写（コピー）・複製、その他著作物の利用については、事前にJPCA（電話03-3812-9424、e-mail:info@e-jpca.net）の許諾を得て下さい。なお、
日本出版著作権協会 無断でコピー・スキャン・デジタル化等の複製をすることは著作権法上
http://www.jpca.jp.net/ での例外を除き、著作権法違反となります。

◆◆◆ 著者略歴 ◆◆◆

松岡 昇（まつおか のぼる）
獨協大学講師、グローバル人材育成コンサルタント。
専門は国際コミュニケーション、社会言語学。『日本人は英語のここが聞き取れない』（アルク）、『会話力がアップする英語雑談75』（DHC）、『桂三輝の英語落語』（共著、アルク）、*Start with Grammar Review for the TOEIC® L&R Test*（共著、松柏社）、『公式TOEIC® Listening & Reading 500+』（制作協力、ETS）など著書多数。大学のほか、企業のコンサルティングや研修、講演も務める。

傍島一夫（そばじま かずお）
イギリスに語学留学後、英会話学校に就職、以降45年以上にわたり英語教育に携わる。著書に *Beat Your Best Score on the TOEIC® L&R Test*（共著、松柏社）、*The Essential Guide to the TOEIC® S&W Tests*（共著、松柏社）、*Start with Grammar Review for the TOEIC® L&R Test*（共著、松柏社）など。現在は、主に企業や大学でTOEIC® L&R対策講座やビジネスライティング講座、英会話講座など、幅広く英語研修を担当している。

One-minute Presentation in English
1分間・英語プレゼンテーション

2017年4月10日　初版第1刷発行
2023年4月10日　初版第4刷発行

著　　者　松岡　昇／傍島一夫
英文校閲　Bill Benfield

発 行 者　森　信久
発 行 所　**株式会社　松 柏 社**
　　　　　〒102-0072　東京都千代田区飯田橋1-6-1
　　　　　TEL 03 (3230) 4813（代表）
　　　　　FAX 03 (3230) 4857
　　　　　http://www.shohakusha.com
　　　　　e-mail: info@shohakusha.com

装　　幀　小島トシノブ（NONdesign）
本文レイアウト・組版　株式会社インターブックス
印刷・製本　シナノ書籍印刷株式会社
ISBN978-4-88198-728-5
略　　号 = 728

Copyright © 2017 by Noboru Matsuoka & Kazuo Sobajima

本書を無断で複写・複製することを禁じます。
落丁・乱丁は送料小社負担にてお取り替え致します。

✦ プレゼンテーション教材にも最適です ✦

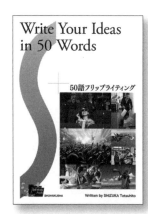

`センテンス⇒パラグラフライティング`

Write Your Ideas in 50 Words
50語フリップライティング

靜 哲人 著

大学生が身近な事柄や日頃感じることを、等身大の視点から「50語程度」の長さで言えるようになるために編纂

■教授資料（解答／試訳）
■教室用CD
●B5判　●全15章65頁　●本体1,700円+税　●略号689

`総合`

Global Leadership Adventures
日本のリアル・トピック20──グローバルな取り組み

Peter Nagano 編著

「グローバリズム」理解に最重要の、企業・エンタメ・芸術・大学・観光などの10項目について自分の意見を言えるようになるための入門テキスト

■教授資料（解答／試訳）
■教室用CD
●B5判　●全20章83頁　●本体1,900円+税　●略号711

`ビデオクリップ`

Getting Personal Using Videoclips: Watch, Listen and Read
大学生のためのビデオクリップ英語総合学習

Clara Birnbaum／高山一郎 著

音楽、言語、ジェンダー、ビル・ゲイツへのインタビューなど豊富なトピックを扱った映像教材

■教授資料（解答／試訳）
■教室用CD
●B5判　●全12章96頁　●本体2,100円+税　●略号618

`パラグラフライティング`

A Guide with Models for Process Writing
モデルで学ぶプロセス・ライティング入門

柴田美紀 著

伝わる英文を書き話せるようになる、日英対訳で練習にも最適なライティング入門

■教授資料（解答／試訳）
●B5判　●全12章120頁　●本体1,950円+税　●略号709

www.shohakusha.com